South Africa's
MOMENT
OF TRUTH

Edgar Lockwood

FRIENDSHIP PRESS • NEW YORK

Library of Congress Cataloging-in-Publication Data

Lockwood, Edgar, 1920-
  South Africa's moment of truth.

  Bibliography: p.
  1. Apartheid—South Africa. 2. Race relations—South Africa.
3. Race Relations—Religious aspects—Christianity. 4. South
Africa—Church history. 1. Title.

DT763.L63 1988   261.8'348'00968—dc19   87-36427
ISBN 0-377-00180-5

Unless otherwise stated, all Bible quotations in this book are from
the Revised Standard Version, copyright 1946 and 1952 by the Division
of Christian Education of the National Council of the Churches of Christ
in the United States of America. Quotations have in certain instances
been edited for inclusive language according to that organization's
guidelines.

Maps drawn by Sean Grandits

We are grateful to authors and publishers who have allowed us to
quote from their books. These permissions are cited in the text; the
books are also listed in the Notes and in "Recent Books" in Chapter
Nine. In addition, we also thank:
  Joseph Lelyveld and Times Books, a Division of Random House,
      for exerpts from *Move Your Shadow: South Africa, Black and White*
      (© Joseph Lelyveld, 1985).
  The Catholic Institute for International Relations and Joseph Hanlon
      for material from *Beggar Your Neighbours: Apartheid Power in Southern
      Africa* (© CIIR, 1986).
  Penguin Books, Ltd., for material from *Mission to South Africa: The
      Commcnwealth Report*, by the Commonwealth Eminent Persons
      Group on South Africa (© The Commonwealth Secretariat, 1986).

ISBN 0-377-00180-5
Editorial Offices: 475 Riverside Drive, Room 772, New York, NY 10115
Distribution Offices: P.0. Box 37844, Cincinnati, OH 45237
Copyright © 1988 Friendship Press, Inc.
Printed in the United States of America

To the countless men, women and children who have offered themselves—and suffered for doing so—in the struggle to bring about a free, democratic and non-racist society in South Africa, this book is dedicated. I have in mind especially those who have died, been imprisoned or been forced into exile because of their courage and commitment. Some, like "Samantha's" aunt, have taught me Christ's compassion even as they denied all connection with the church. Others, like John, belonged to religious orders and were willing to lose a limb rather than to deny that they saw Christ in the face of a political refugee. Some were heavily political and others were just concerned, human people forced by the situation to be political in spite of themselves. But then, as George Bernanos's country priest said, "Does it matter? Grace is everywhere."

Foreword

The struggle for justice in South Africa is not a local affair: it is everyone's struggle. Humanity's future will be shaped by decisions made in this conflict. The power confrontation is not merely a confrontation between black and white in South Africa, but between oppressor and oppressed, between justice and injustice, and between obedience to God and to the idolatry of power. It is a hard theological struggle. The meaning of faithfulness and faithlessness are here exposed.

It is important that the long history of the many dimensions of the struggle be understood by people both in and out of South Africa. In particular, people of the Church worldwide need to develop a sense of solidarity with us so that the world may know that when one member of Christ's Church suffers, all suffer together. Those who share a common pain will also share a common hope. The future will be a new "life together."

Ted Lockwood has taken great pains to amass a great deal of information and to present it to the reader in intelligent and understandable fashion. We in South Africa are indebted to him for his effort and we appreciate the opportunity it provides for common purpose and mutual participation in the struggle for love and justice.

— Allan A. Boesak

The Rev. Dr. Allan A. Boesak is moderator of the N.G. Sendingkerk (Dutch Reformed Mission Church), the denomination in which he serves as pastor of the Bellville Sendingkerk in Cape Town, South Africa. He is also senior vice president of the South African Council of Churches, president of the World Alliance of Reformed Churches, and a patron of the United Democratic Front.

Acknowledgements

In writing this book, I have benefitted enormously from the scholarly work of so many people that it is impossible to thank them all as handsomely as they deserve. The list of recent books (page 172) indicates some of my debt to those from whom I have learned and borrowed so much.

A number of knowledgeable and dedicated friends have taken time to read and review the manuscript. I am particularly grateful to Jennifer Davis, Bud Day, Larry Gilley, Bill Johnston, Bill Minter, Ruth Minter and Carol Thompson, who made valuable suggestions for improving style, coherence, interpretation and balance. The text also received the careful scrutiny of the publications committee of Friendship Press. Their comments were extremely helpful in revising the original draft. None of these consultants should be held responsible for the final result; I and my editors are the ones to receive the blame or praise.

I have been blessed with perceptive and talented editors at Friendship Press. Nadine Hundertmark persuaded me to undertake the project and gave me important understanding and encouragement in the early stages of writing. When Nadine went on leave to give birth to a child, Carol Ames took over editing the revised text with the assistance of copy editor Laura Mol. They have read the text with fresh eyes, keeping ordinary readers uppermost in their minds. They pointed out places overloaded with unnecessary details, rephrased awkward sentences, and forced me to explain facts that needed more attention. And so I thank all my editors. I found them reasonable, tractable and perceptive. Not knowledgeable themselves about southern Africa, they were the perfect cure for alleged expertise that makes the truth obscure and unlovable.

I wrote this book while serving as the part-time interim pastor of my parish, St. Stephen and the Incarnation Episcopal Church, in Washington, D.C. I am grateful to my fellow parishioners for their love and understanding in helping me survive with honor the stresses of doing two jobs simultaneously.

Finally, I thank my wife, Dianne, who read several chapters and made valuable comments. While I was busy with the book, she often seemed to have lost a husband. I thank her for her forbearance and love when I was heavily preoccupied with reading, research and writing.

Contents

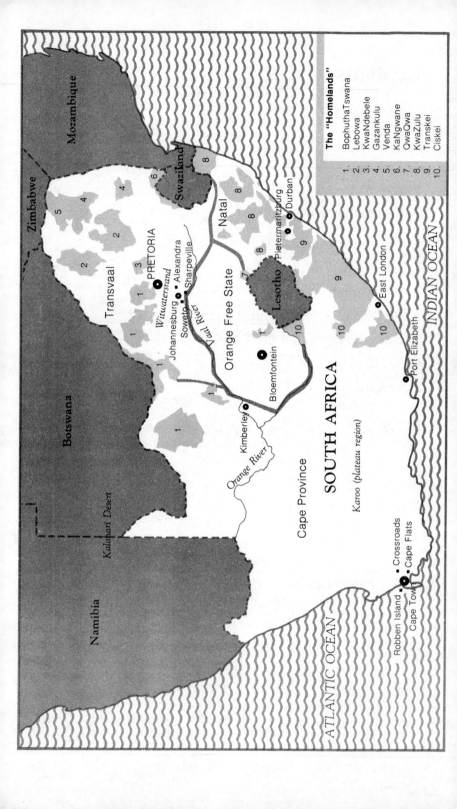

The "Homelands"

1. BophuthaTswana
2. Lebowa
3. KwaNdebele
4. Gazankulu
5. Venda
6. KaNgwane
7. QwaQwa
8. KwaZulu
9. Transkei
10. Ciskei

SOUTH AFRICA

Namibia

Botswana

Zimbabwe

Mozambique

Swaziland

Lesotho

Kalahari Desert

Transvaal

PRETORIA
Witwatersrand
Johannesburg · Alexandra
Soweto ■ Sharpeville
Vaal River

Orange Free State

Bloemfontein

Kimberley
Orange River

Natal

Pietermaritzburg
Durban

East London

Port Elizabeth

INDIAN OCEAN

Cape Province

Karoo (plateau region)

Robben Island ·■ Crossroads
Cape Town ·■ Cape Flats

ATLANTIC OCEAN

Chapter One:
Crisis and Kairos

The time has come. The moment of truth has arrived. South Africa has been plunged into a crisis that is shaking the foundations and there is every indication that the crisis has only just begun and that it will deepen and become even more threatening in the months to come. It is the KAIROS or moment of truth not only for apartheid but also for the church. . . . For very many Christians in South Africa this is...the moment of grace and opportunity.... It is a dangerous time because, if this opportunity is missed, and allowed to pass by, the loss for the Church, for the Gospel and for all the people of South Africa will be immeasurable. . . .

A crisis is a judgment that brings out the best in some people and the worst in others. It is a moment of truth that shows us up for what we really are. [From *The Kairos Document*, September 1985.]

No one in North America who has been reading the newspapers or watching the evening news over the past few years can fail to be aware that there is indeed a crisis in South Africa.

A spiral of violence has been escalating

On our television screens we have seen troops and police shooting down unarmed demonstrators, even attacking certain funeral processions.

Since the most recent government declaration of a state of emergency in June 1986 to the present writing—a period of only ten months—some 25,000 people have been placed in detention. Thousands continue to be held without trial or chance of judicial review. They are being detained because they hold opinions that the South African government believes to be dangerous, even if those holding the opinions are still children. The government admits to having detained 279 children between 11 and 15 years of age in order to combat "revolutionary-inspired crime"—and this admission does not cover the detention of the much larger number of young people aged 15 to 18. According to the Detainees' Parents Support Committee, a civil rights group, 2,000 to 3,000 juveniles between the ages of 9 and 18 are being held (as of April 1987).

Those who have been detained are of course not only children, but also many others who are simply trying to help those who suffer: social workers who advise clients with legal or other problems, doctors who have treated people hurt in police actions, lawyers, journalists, and clergy seeking to visit parishioners. Many who have been detained know first-hand that the South African police routinely and systematically use torture to extract information.

Western media play up what they say is a new element of violence: blacks attacking blacks, in some cases using such brutal tactics as "necklaces" (gasoline-doused rubber tires put around the victim's neck and set alight).

Guerillas trained and supported by the outlawed African National Congress (ANC) continue to infiltrate South Africa, placing land mines along country roads and bombs in the cities. At the same time, South African troops raid neighboring countries that the Pretoria government accuses of harboring ANC fighters.

Outspoken church leaders like Desmond Tutu and Allan Boesak have become household names in North America. But millions of Christians less well-known are also involved in the fight against apartheid and are just as important for us to know about.

A clamor of voices

As concerned Christian people, we hear confusing and contradictory calls upon us.

We hear calls for peace and nonviolence, calls to stop cold-blooded murder, whether that killing is carried out by the government or by African youth. We hear calls for dialogue between the parties, but no one seems prepared to talk and we wonder why not.

We hear calls for action to punish or isolate South Africa through trade sanctions and divestment of stock in North American corporations doing business there. At the same time, we also hear that divestment will only harm the African people whom it is supposed to benefit. Or that, if isolated, South Africa will only turn up the heat of repression and become even more immune to outside influence.

We hear increasing acceptance of the idea that a prolonged and bloody civil war is the probable—or even necessary—consequence of the present stalemate. In this view, the conflict has become so polarized so that neutrality, mediation or compromise seem out of the question; the time has come to side either with apartheid or with the liberation movements that are determined to abolish apartheid.

The crisis calls North American Christians to understand the choices that churchpeople in that distant country, South Africa, are facing. South African Christians are asking for our support. We must ask how best we can help. The choices are difficult; they may seem remote from our lives. Yet we are unable to avoid such decisions because, as St. Paul pointed out, we are all members of One Body and are already inextricably connected in Christ.

The foundations of South African society have indeed been shaken. The hopes of the majority of South Africans for a just, democratic and non-racist society seem closer to fulfillment than ever. Yet the hopes of the majority are also the fears of the privileged minority.

However far away South Africa may seem, the issues in that land are the same ones facing us North Americans. On our continent, racism has experienced a resurgence. Our churches largely continue to be segregated institutions. In the United States in particular, many black people are also experiencing violence, unemployment, homelessness and the destruction of community—all amid a relatively prosperous society.

In relation to our foreign policies, the South African situation represents the world in microcosm. Like the governing minority in South Africa, the United States, Canada and other developed countries of European origin enjoy a disproportionate share of the world's wealth, income and power. This dominant position, so some analysts argue, is built on the underdevelopment and exploitation of parts of the world that contain the majority of the world's population—and that majority is not white.

The crisis seen through a thousand eyes:
Samantha

My dearest Aunt,
Hi, or should I say, I greet you in the name of all those

children who have died under the hands of the police and all those who have endured pain, torture and suffering during these months of unrest.

Samantha* is sixteen years old and has been living in Cape Town. She is a member of a well-known "Indian" family, some of whom have been part of the political opposition to apartheid and some of whom have not. Samantha's parents tend to be afraid of politics. Her aunt, however, has been forced into exile because of the active work she has done as a lawyer and a member of the African National Congress, the oldest and largest African liberation movement, which has been outlawed by the government since 1960.

Samantha tells her aunt of the careful, disciplined political work in her own school:

Throughout, schools began fighting for democratic SRCs [Student Representative Councils].

Mass meetings were organized. It was at these meetings that we became aware of the trouble in the places away from us. Representatives from each school gave a report back of the goings on. . . . Many schools marched since they did not have the necessary bus fare . . . students were dispersed and baton-charged . . . students from Mitchells Plain area were rocked out of the buses by police and then beaten. . . .

During the fourth week most of the teachers in the western Cape met for a mass meeting in Rylands. A police informer was found. . . . They caught, disarmed and sent him on his way. He returned minutes later with three casspirs [armored personnel carriers] and about twelve police vans.

Dr. Boesak[†] always stresses discipline but some of these students never listen. After two meetings that I attended, students gathered and marched to other schools to disrupt their lessons. . . . The spirit amongst the students grew stronger with every child being beaten and arrested. . . .

During the fifth week Dr. Boesak announced the march to Pollsmoor.[‡] For the past few days I was wondering whether

---

* Samantha is a real person but "Samantha" is not her real name. To identify her or to name her aunt's whereabouts might endanger them.
† Allan Boesak, president of the World Alliance of Reformed Churches and an ordained minister of the so-called "Coloured" branch of the Dutch Reformed Church.
‡ The prison where Nelson Mandela, the most prominent leader of the African National Congress, is serving a life sentence; see Chapter Two, page 38.

I should go or not. I had to choose between getting beaten, arrested and shot or living with a terrible conscience. Mom did not make my decision any easier. She was more scared than I was.

Samantha did indeed go to the great gathering at Athlone Stadium, but the authorities had banned it. So when the people arrived, the police were also there. When the police began to attack, the crowd of 4,000 began to march in groups of five toward Pollsmoor Prison. Samantha describes what happened next:

Marshalls controlled a peaceful and orderly crowd. Before we entered the area for whites we were stopped by two casspirs. The priests and nuns leading the march were arrested after police fired teargas onto a seated crowd. . . .

The entire area was cordoned off, so we had to dodge the police cars. Once you are out there and you are between the ages of 13 and 20, they arrest you. . . . We were standing about six metres away from the police, now armed with sjamboks [whips], and I did not know whether to move or just be still. . . .

We had to dodge three police vans. . . . They got up and started firing at two innocent women. . . . The air was filled with teargas. . . .

Botha* and his empty promises! He wants law and order and yet he declared a state of emergency. . . . He wants to create peace and yet policemen dressed in riot gear are allowed to provoke the students into throwing stones at them. . . . How can students be blamed for burning buses once they have seen their parents or brothers and sisters being beaten before their eyes?

Instead of things slowing down a bit, as the goverment thought it would, violence is increasing. More and more children group together. . . . Botha's regime thinks that by taking away our leaders they are breaking our spirit; don't they realize that for every one person taken or beaten, ten more stand to show their solidarity? By the leaders being detained, the only thing [left] is a disorderly crowd. . . . Boesak is what Mandela was many years back. The people respect him and follow him whole-heartedly. This is something that the government can't expect to vanish once they lock him up.

---
* P. W. Botha, the State President of South Africa.

[Samantha's letter is dated August 29, 1985. We are grateful to her aunt for permission to use it.]

Jacobus Steyn

Jacobus Steyn[*] is what South African's call a *verkrampte*, an Afrikaner nationalist of the strict school. He is a respected physician in a country town in the Cape Province:

From the earliest of times there was a difference between the English and the Afrikaners. And after the [Anglo-Boer] war, it was the English, more or less, who ruled the country. We felt, I suppose, as the Coloureds feel today. We had to battle to prove ourselves. . . . I tell my kids about the war. I take them to visit the concentration camps [run by the British during the Anglo-Boer War of 1899-1902]. I am proud to show them how our people suffered.

My grandfather was deported to Ceylon, and my grandmother was in one of the camps. . . . My grandmother would tell me how women and children who slept next to her—whose warmth and life she felt—would be dead when she woke up in the morning. There were days that they were given nothing to eat. The milk of nursing mothers ran dry. There was no medicine, no doctors, no sanitation.

Jacobus Steyn believes that he holds no grudges against the English and that whites, whether they be English or Afrikaner, should be united against the militant white "leftists" and be firm as far as the Black and "Coloured" people are concerned:

Oh, we have problems, but I think we have a future. . . . Time is running out for the white man. If we don't take a stand together, then we'll go under. . . . We are prepared to share the country—territorial segregation, as we have done with the homelands. . . . But I'm not prepared to let my culture go by letting those people take over. Sorry. I'll be in South Africa until they take over. If they are going to take over, the majority, then I'll leave. I'll never be able to sit here and be ruled by the Black man. . . .

I see you are still having problems in America putting Blacks and whites together in school. I mean they are forced together, and that is bad. These things must be faced. But, of course,

---

[*] Not his real name.

there are certain leaders who like to force things down another nation's throat. . . .

It is actually the extreme whites who are trying to push the Blacks into being militant.

The interviewer asks: Do you see Black participation in the government as a possibility?

No, I'm sorry.

Interviewer: And Coloured participation?

The Coloureds might . . . a qualified franchise where the educated Coloureds would join the white man in certain respects. [A qualified franchise would make the right to vote conditional on proof that the voter had attained a certain level of education.]

. . . We mustn't be rushed, and the world is rushing us. They need to preach to other people what they themselves should have done.

Hennie van der Merve

Hennie van der Merve* is an Afrikaner of a different sort from Jacobus Steyn. He might be described by the Afrikaans term *verlicte* (enlightened person), someone who has traveled and seen a bit of the world and who believes that new solutions must be found to the problems of South Africa.

Hennie comes from a family of "trekkers," Dutch settlers who traveled far inland from the coast of South Africa in search of new lands and occupations. His forebears revolted against British colonial domination; his father fought the British in the Boer War. After the war was over, however, he taught his children that they must live with the English, learn their language and be educated with them. Hennie's marriage to Rose, a devout English woman, eventually led him to an experience which he calls "becoming a real Christian" and an Anglican priest. That makes him "a renegade, an apostate" to Afrikaners, he says. To break from the South African Dutch Reformed Church to which most Afrikaners belongs and to join an English-speaking church was almost to lose one's identity, as Hennie explains: "You really can't separate the Afrikaner from his religion. It is almost like the Jews. You are a Jew by birth and by religion."

In his first parish in Rhodesia (then a white-settler-run country north of South Africa, now called Zimbabwe), Hennie ran into

---

* Not his real name.

trouble. When Rhodesia declared its independence from Britain, defying British and other international calls for democratic rule by the black majority, Hennie refused to bless the new flag. "They hated my guts for that," he says. When his parishioners came with leftover food to give to the poor, he insisted that they actually see how Africans lived:

> I took them into some of the houses. "Look how close together they live," I said. "You allow them to be poor, but you don't allow more than one person in a grave. These people here are living closer together than they would be if they were in a grave. You tell me you understand them because you speak their language. But you don't know how they live. You can't tell me you know them. You can't make decisions for them."

> We grow up without knowing the other. That is one of our major problems. It has got much worse in the last thirty years or so with apartheid. Previously we had lived closer together. We had no choice. We knew how they lived. . . . We must learn to see things from the other man's point of view. We must feel his agony. We must get involved at quite a different level. Ultimately this getting to know the other man is the only thing that will save us.

> *The interviewer reflects on Hennie's views:*
> Even a man as open-minded as Hennie, I thought to myself, cannot bring himself to say simply that the Blacks should be given the vote and freedom of movement. Was Hennie's commitment to the Coloureds a way of avoiding the Black problem? He often seemed indifferent to the Blacks. Like other whites in the Cape, he claimed not to know them and could, therefore, safely ignore them. Hennie went on to talk about the horrors of apartheid, the breaking up of families through reclassification and immigration, and eventually—he seemed to talk himself into it—the legal status of Blacks.

> *The interviewer quotes Hennie:*
> Our system is unacceptable. We offer no alternative. . . . The government has to face facts. They must train a responsible leadership. They can't go on arresting, detaining, and banning every African leader who surfaces. Then you will have no one to negotiate with when the time to negotiate comes. And it will come.

[We are grateful to Dr. Vincent Crapanzano and Random House for allowing us to quote from his interviews with "Jacobus Steyn" and "Hennie van der Merwe" in his book, *Waiting*.]

Johanna Molutsi

Johanna Molutsi's life shows the path that many black South Africans have followed from the country to the city in search of jobs and education—of whatever sort they can find. She grew up on land that her grandfather farmed north of Pretoria. Her grandfather did not own the land. It was adjacent to a Christian Zion Apostolic Church[*] of which he was the pastor.

> We suffer that place—we had to suffer there. . . . We were planting. You know, I never went to school. I don't know the school. My sister Lydia doesn't know the school. Myself, I am better because I can write a little bit.

Only when Johanna was fifteen and began to work as a domestic servant did she learn to write by copying the schoolwork of her employer's children:

> I'm interested in everything. You can just show me something and I just do it the same time. So I learnt to write my name and so on. Then I find I know how to write. When I read the paper people say I am a mistress.[†] I can read anything. God gave me to learn because I was interested with the children.

Life on the farm was hard. Johanna learned how to plant and plow when she was ten. When her grandfather remarried, his new wife favored her own children over Johanna and her sister, who were orphans. Because her grandfather would not let her keep any of the money she earned, Johanna ran away to work for some poor white people in Norwood:

> They pay me ten shillings a month.[‡] I work hard washing, ironing, cleaning lots. I knew just a few words—tea I know what it is and coffee. They eat porridge with meat, like me. They like cabbage and potatoes and they like green beans

---

[*] A black African independent church that emphasizes healing and the gifts of the Spirit.

[†] Johanna means that people saw that she was just as literate as the woman who employed her.

[‡] About $2.50 (U.S.) in those days.

and potatoes—they were mixing it. They had to give me a blanket. They had to give me a dress.

In time, she found better work and also got pregnant:

I don't know how I got pregnant. I was very shy. I was just crying all the time. Before, he was a nice man, but after, he got a lot of girls. We were still stupid to go after him and he just drop you.

Johanna kept her daughter, Leah, with her for a year and then left the child with her aunt and her grandfather, with whom she had become reconciled.

Eventually she married Jacob Molutsi, who was employed at a high class grocery and delicatessen. Johanna made baby clothes for a woman who sold them to a department store. Both the Molutsis were thrifty, and soon they felt they had a lot of money. So they opened a cafe in Alexandra, an African township, where Johanna cooked and sold food. At first the couple were happy with their money, which they shared as needed. But after a time, the same pattern emerged that had existed with her grandfather.

He wanted to work his own side, but he say it's community of property. He wanted all the money, even now. He doesn't drink. He doesn't know what to do with the money. He works, I work. . . . He buys cars, he buys suits, doesn't buy me nothing. I don't care. . . .

I thought when he grows old he'll be better. Now he's *worse*. He fight with me for nothing and I don't die. He kills me, I don't die. . . . I can't understand why God let me to this. I like to die. God doesn't want to take me.

In her old age, Johanna's church, the African Episcopal Church, is the comfort and solace of her life. She is a member of the church committee and wears a handsome hat and cape, which are badges of office. When her husband consults the traditional African healers and practitioners of "witchcraft," she fears that they will conspire to cause her harm; only her faith in God makes her confident that they are powerless to hurt her:

If God doesn't will those people to do what they like, they won't do me nothing. When I die he'll just get my body, he won't catch my soul.

[Excerpts from the story of Johanna Molutsi are quoted from *A Talent for Tomorrow: Life Stories of South African Servants*, with the permission of author Suzanne Gordon and Ravan Press.]

Carl Niehaus

In December 1983, Carl Niehaus and his fiancee, Jansie Lourens, were tried and convicted of high treason. Carl was sentenced to fifteen years imprisonment and Jansie to four for doing what their consciences told them was right. Carl is an Afrikaner and a Christian. He was brought up in South Africa's Dutch Reformed Church. Carl told the court:

Christianity has always played an active and important role in my life. I have always been actively involved in church affairs—so much so that I decided to join the ministry.

His dream of going into the ministry was shattered, however, when he was expelled from the Rand Afrikaans University for putting up posters calling for the release from prison of Nelson Mandela (the African National Congress leader). After his expulsion, Carl worked at a community center in Alexandra township.

Here I had the privilege of being confronted with the shocking conditions which face the people living in the township. I realized what life in South Africa was really all about. People were suffering from the injustices of the influx control, migrant labour and pass law systems.

Because of government policies they were being forced to return to the homelands where they were dying of malnutrition. The people were being forced to leave the land of their birth to go to drought-stricken areas where they had no hope of employment.

I as a Christian could not condone these policies and after a considerable amount of turmoil in my own soul I decided to become an active supporter of the African National Congress.[1]

The apartheid policy is a heresy and I believe the church should move towards a state of confession, and no longer participate in the Government, its policies or its military wing, the South African Defense Force.[2]

A Catholic laywoman recalls the trial:

The testimony of one young man, Lionel Murcott, stands out in my mind. Lionel is an artist and a poet, sensitive and with an intense sense of the importance of personal integrity. He is also a deeply committed Christian, an Anglican. He spoke with transparent honesty. Among other things, he described how he and Carl distributed leaflets entitled "Stand up to the oppressors," by putting them under the [windshield] wipers of cars parked in a Rand Easter Show parking lot. . . . The pamphlets encouraged young men to refuse to undergo the compulsory military training that all young white men are required to do. Such encouragement is a serious crime in South Africa.[3]

Another friend of Carl's refused to testify against him. Father Timothy Stanton, an "apolitical" Anglican priest, had known Carl as a student at the University of Witwatersrand. Father Stanton told the court:

I believe that to make a statement, or to give any evidence against Carl Niehaus, would violate my conscience.

I can say that he is my friend, although in fact I don't know him very well. I have no idea what he has done or is supposed to have done to warrant this charge.

But I believe in him. I believe he is concerned to bring about a more just ordering of society than exists here at present.

I would rather live in jail as a result of an empty gesture made in good faith, than outside it with a guilty conscience.[4]

Stanton served six months in jail under South Africa's Internal Security Act for refusing to testify.

Another "friend" of Carl's was Robert Whitecross, who as a Bachelor of Commerce student at the university had become close to Carl. Whitecross had made a reconnaissance of the local gas works and had identified positions from which strategic photos could be taken. Perhaps the ANC would be interested. So Rob and Carl went down and took photos together. What Carl didn't know was that Robert Whitecross was Warrant Officer Whitecross of the Security Police. Nor did he realize that Whitecross had stationed police photographers so that they could take pictures of Carl photographing the gas works.

Rob was not a friend. He was an enemy, whose entrapment and subsequent testimony clinched the government's case.[5]

[The account of Carl Niehaus's case is taken from newspaper reports and personal letters.]

Frank Chikane

Christian Greetings,
I have been instructed by the West Rand District Commit-tee to write you this letter. The Committee has suspended you from the 6th August, 1981, for the following reason: that you are still active in politics, but on the 31st of January, 1980, you promised the Committee to stay away from politics. The Committee found that you are still appearing in the newspapers.
Yours in His Service,
V.F. Pietersee, Chairman

The Rev. Frank Chikane, to whom this letter was addressed, was a black South African pastor in the white-led Apostolic Faith Mission. He explained his conflict with his church to author and National Public Radio reporter, Julie Frederikse, in this way:

[The people in leadership of my church] claim that their position is such that they do not participate in the political issues of the country, that they are neutral as a church. . . . I urged that the church must be involved in the South African problem, that we must guide the people, that we cannot just leave them to face the bloodbath that is coming. [I say bloodbath] Because in the history of struggles, a ruling class has never voluntarily given in. It is only when you produce power equal to theirs that they start thinking and talking. . . . So, from the point of view of the oppressed, [the black people of South Africa] are saying, "We have tried everything else and the only thing left to do is to match the power that the oppressor has got." It is the violence of the state that keeps the state in power, so people feel that to match that power you must also use the same method.

The church authorities felt that the South African government's policy of separate development could work if given a chance. They also felt since Chikane had been detained four times between 1978 and 1982, he must be in the wrong.

Well, I get detained because I differ with the state, I'm critical of them. . . . These guys [the security police] simply come during the night without an appointment, so I can't control it. . . .[The church leaders] felt, well they cannot have such a person in their church, so they suspended me. . . . Actually, my feeling is now that in South Africa today, those kind of Christians [who claim not to be political] have become more dangerous—or at least they are more prone to cause people to resort to unfortunate methods—than non-Christians.

If Christians can say those things that [the police] were saying about Christianity—that the Bible has nothing to do with blacks, the Bible only talks about whites—well, then you can understand why so many blacks feel so negative about Christianity. I remember the police tried to threaten me. . . . "We don't want to hear anything from your Bible."

. . . I had to tell them that everything I did—even if it was against the government—I did because of my commitment as a Christian. So I could not explain anything I had done without calling on the Scriptures to reveal my position.

Although the local church board and 600 residents of Kagiso, the township where he lived, asked for his reinstatement, Chikane decided not to fight his church superiors any longer, and he took a position as director of the Institute for Contextual Theology in Johannesburg. Chikane, who has recently been elected general secretary of the South African Council of Churches, feels that the church needs a new theology that springs from deep engagement in people's struggle for freedom and equality:

The new methodology means becoming involved in the struggle for a full humanity—in squatter camps, in makeshift shacks, in the ghettoes of South Africa, and in the barren and arid lands of the bantustans* where people are dying of hunger and diseases. It involves being in detention with the victims of the system where one will be forced to ask realistic and concrete theological questions about God. When one starts asking seemingly heretical questions about the role of God in all this, one starts to "do theology." This demands cost. It is demanding because it means theologians must relinquish their position of privilege and choose rather

---

* "Bantustans" are the so-called "homelands" to which black South Africans are assigned, supposedly by tribal background. (See Chapter Four, page 56.)

to suffer with the people of God: from this experience a
people's theology can be born.

[The interview excerpt is taken from *South Africa: A Different Kind
of War*, with the kind permission of Julie Frederikse. The final
quotation is from an essay by Chikane in *Reistance and Hope, South
African Essays in Honor of Beyers Naude*, edited by Charles Villa-
Vicencio and John W. de Gruchy; published in the U.S. by Wm.
B. Eerdmans and in South Africa by David Philip Ltd.]

Is Christ Divided?

As these six portraits illustrate, a time of crisis calls forth different
responses from different individuals. Yet all read the same Bible
and all claim to be part of one tradition. As the crisis intensifies
and as government censorship tries to keep South Africans and
the whole world from knowing what is happening in the country,
the churches are reaching out to one another for common
understanding of the work God calls them to take up and for
collective strength to accomplish it. The church itself has become
an arena of revolutionary conflict, in which calls are issued in
the name of God to join the oppressed in their fight for liberation.
South Africa's Dutch Reformed Church, to which Jacobus Steyn
belongs, has begun to acknowledge that apartheid has no biblical
foundation, yet local segregation remains the rule. Even the
apolitical churches like the one that Johanna Molutsi belongs to
are now being drawn into the struggle and being divided in the
process.

Is there only one legitimate position? If the church is to decide
for liberation, then are any means that lead toward that goal
appropriate, as Frank Chikane seems to be arguing?

Before we take up these theological questions toward the end
of this book, it will help to become familiar with how South Africa
reached its present impasse. In doing so, we will have to leave
out much that the reader who is willing to delve into details wants
to know. (Suggestions for further study will be found in the books
section of Chapter Nine and in *Until We Are Free*, a study guide
to this book.) A brief history may, however, furnish us with the
lens we need to focus on the present situation.

Chapter Two:
A History Written in Blood

> To legitimate the policy of apartheid. . . the mythology
> presents the African inhabitants as a totally distinct sub-
> species of humanity. They are deemed to have arrived in
> South Africa no earlier than the first Dutch settlers and to
> have blindly resisted the spread of "civilization," which is
> regarded as an exclusively "White" and "Christian" achieve-
> ment. . . . Afrikaners were a Chosen People with a God-
> given destiny. [Leonard Thompson, *The Political Mythology of
> Apartheid*, p. 29]

If we are to make sense out of what is now happening in South
Africa, we have to understand its history by listening as carefully
as we can to the story of all its people. We have to sift out the
false mythology and look for the historical realities.

Early times: the hunter-gatherers

Drawings found on cave walls bear silent witness to the earliest
inhabitants of southern Africa, the Khoi-San. Thousands of years
before the birth of Christ, they roamed the grasslands, marshlands
and deserts living a semi-nomadic life. The Khoi-San were short,
slight people with a yellowish-brown complexion. They ate wild
plants, fruits and nuts plus birds, rodents and lizards. To
supplement this meager diet they sometimes hunted deer and
antelope and even giraffes and hippos, using poisoned spears and
arrows.

Because hunting required great strength, awareness and courage,
the hunters prepared themselves carefully with medicine and
religious ceremonies. Like North American native peoples, the
Khoi-San respected the spirits of the animals which they hunted.
They also believed in a Great Spirit.

The Khoi-San lived in small bands of a few families, moving
from camp to camp following the animals. They did not need a
political organization beyond the hunting band itself. Each member

of the band had to live cooperatively and share common tasks. They had few possessions, and few quarrels over money or property. Today, a remnant of the Khoi-San people still follows some of their ancient ways in the deserts of Botswana and Namibia.

The herders

At some point, perhaps two thousand years ago, some of the Khoi-San took up herding sheep and, later, cattle, which they probably got by trading with Bantu-speaking people to the north. These herder clans learned to make pottery. They drank the sour milk from their animals and sometimes killed them for meat. The Khoi-Khoi, as this herder group of Khoi-San came to be called, settled at first along the Orange and Vaal Rivers. Later, a sub-group called the Nama went west to the Atlantic. Namibia gets its name from the Nama people.[1]

It was, however, on the western and southern coasts of the Cape of Good Hope that water and pasture were best and land was most abundant. There the Cape Khoi-Khoi prospered and developed their own culture, living in clans under a hereditary headman. They built better houses than their ancestors had done and, with better food, the Khoi-Khoi grew bigger and healthier than the Khoi-San hunters.

The languages of the Khoi-San and Khoi-Khoi included "clicks" made with the tongue. Later these were adapted into other African languages such as Xhosa and Zulu. Early European settlers called the click speakers "Hottentots" from a dance-chant word. The click language seemed so grotesque to the settlers that it led them to speculate that the Khoi-Khoi were descended from monkeys. "Hottentot" became a synonym for "brute" or "boor" in Europe in the next three centuries.

The Bantu-speakers arrive in South Africa

To the north and east, an iron age civilization was created by a dark-skinned negroid people who spoke languages called "Bantu."[*] In the Transvaal, archeologists have discovered Iron-Age pottery dating from the third to the sixth centuries A.D. Similar finds in Natal, the Transkei and Ciskei are dated later but also clearly show that people with an Iron-Age culture were present

---

[*] Bantu languages share a noun similar to *ntu* for "person" and a prefix similar to *ba* for that class of nouns.

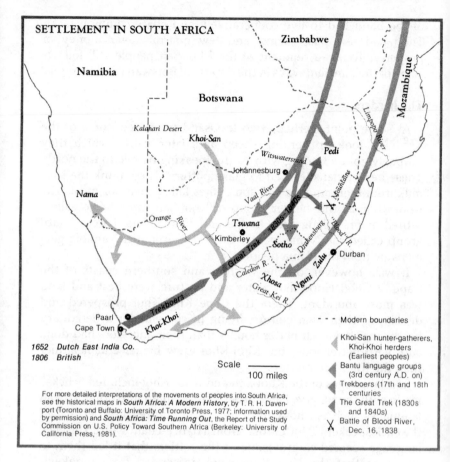

SETTLEMENT IN SOUTH AFRICA

Zimbabwe

Namibia

Botswana

Kalahari Desert

Khoi-San

Nama

Pedi

Witswatersrand

Johannesburg

Orange River

Vaal River

Tswana

Kimberley

Sotho

Great Trek 1830s-1840s

Drakensburg

Caledon R.

Xhosa

Great Kei R.

Nguni

Zulu

Durban

Blood R.

Limpopo River

Mozambique

Mountains

Trekboers

Paarl

Cape Town

Khoi-Khoi

1652   Dutch East India Co.
1806   British

Scale
100 miles

– – – Modern boundaries

Khoi-San hunter-gatherers,
Khoi-Khoi herders
(Earliest peoples)

Bantu language groups
(3rd century A.D. on)

Trekboers (17th and 18th
centuries

The Great Trek (1830s
and 1840s)

X   Battle of Blood River,
Dec. 16, 1838

For more detailed interpretations of the movements of peoples into South Africa,
see the historical maps in *South Africa: A Modern History*, by T. R. H. Davenport (Toronto and Buffalo: University of Toronto Press, 1977; information used
by permission) and *South Africa: Time Running Out*, the Report of the Study
Commission on U.S. Policy Toward Southern Africa (Berkeley: University of
California Press, 1981).

in what is now South Africa long before the Europeans
"discovered" that part of the world.

The ability to shape iron tools meant that the people of these
groups were able to cultivate grain for a staple diet, while also
drinking the milk and eating the meat of goats, sheep and cattle.
Because cultivation of the soil eventually exhausted its fertility,
from time to time farmers had to search for better soil, moving
their villages and rebuilding their clay and thatch houses.

As time went on, the Iron-Age societies grew larger and more
complex. During the rainy season everyone farmed, but soon
occupations developed for other times of year. In the dry season,
men worked in mines or as iron and copper smiths. Women became
expert potters, matweavers and tailors. At Palaborwa, in the
northeast Transvaal region, copper was mined continuously for

a thousand years. Gold and tin were mined in the Transvaal. Smelters alloyed copper and tin to make bronze. Trade sprang up with the outside world along the southeast coast of Africa; African metals, skins and ivory were sold for use first in Asia and later in Europe. Some African clans along the trade routes became rich and grew into powerful chiefdoms, governing large areas.

The Nguni

Along the eastern coast, between the Drakensberg mountains and the sea, abundant and reliable rainfall makes the land more suitable for crops than in most areas to the west. This area therefore attracted a large group of the Bantu speakers called the Nguni, who settled in what is now Swaziland, southern Mozambique and the Natal province of South Africa.

When disputes arose within a clan, dissidents tended to move south and form their own clan. By 1600 the Xhosa clan of the Nguni had settled near the Kei River, where they came into contact with Khoi-Khoi herders. Although similar in culture and political structure, the Nguni people farmed more land and raised larger families than the neighboring Khoi-Khoi herders. They therefore tended to become politically dominant as well. The Nguni forced the Khoi-San hunters to migrate further west to the fringes of the mountains and the plateaus.

In the eighteenth century, tensions began to rise among the northern Nguni. One cause of tension was the rising power of chiefdoms that controlled trade with the outside world. Chiefs like Zwide of the Ndwandwe and Dingiswayo of the Mthethwa increased their power and wealth by organizing and controlling elephant hunting, exports of ivory and imports of cloth, beads and metal. They forced other clans to accept their monopolies.

Another cause of tension was population growth. Nguni farmers started to grow maize (a plant imported from South America by the Portuguese), doubling their grain crops. But maize requires good rains and when drought came, food shortages led to wars. The Ndwandwe and Mthethwa chiefdoms began to raid and conquer other chiefdoms and to mold them into new, centralized kingdoms.

The Tswana/Sotho

Further west, on the great plateau between the Orange and the Limpopo rivers, lived the people called Tswana and their cousins the Sotho. The most northern group of the Tswana/Sotho were the Pedi. As in the Nguni region, trade laid the foundation of a powerful kingdom. The Pedi king ruled over a confederation of chieftaincies which paid tribute to him. Although he kept no standing army, he had a system of disciplined regiments of young men and women who could be called on for national service.

South of the Pedi kingdom lay the city-states of the Tswana, which were built in the Witwatersrand area as early as the thirteenth century. Stone-walled towns and villages were set in the midst of agricultural lands and cattle posts. Tswana kings built up their states through control of cattle ownership and profits from mining, manufacturing and trade.

From the sixteenth century on, Tswana chiefdoms spread west into the edge of the Kalahari desert while others went south across the Vaal or Lekwa to found the Sotho chiefdoms.

As elsewhere, periodic drought made feeding a growing population difficult, and conflicts arose. Beginning in the late eighteenth century, the Tswana states increasingly fought with one another over agricultural land, pastures and control over trade with the coasts.[3]

Mfecane / Difaqane (the Crushing)

The worst fighting was still to come. In the terrible wars of the 1820s and 1830s, called the *Mfecane* in Zulu, or *Difaqane* in Sotho or Tswana, the states and the people were crushed like grain in a mill.

The wars began with the rise to power of a new kind of king, who built a centralized military dictatorship. Shaka was the chief of a clan called the Zulu under Dingiswayo, king of the Mthethwa people. Following the death of Dingiswayo in battle, Shaka seized power. Like Napoleon of France a few years earlier, Shaka built a strong, highly disciplined army that was personally loyal to him as commander-in-chief. He replaced the thrown spear with a short stabbing sword and a large cowhide shield. With their shields locked together, an advancing line of Zulu warriors was safe against thrown spears. At short range, their swords were deadly. Shaka saw that his new breed of soldiers were well-fed and catered to. With this standing army, Shaka conquered most of the surrounding Nguni chiefdoms. The chiefs became his *indunas*, royal agents, responsible only to him and without constituencies of their own.

One of these indunas, Mzilikazi of the Khumalo clan, revolted but then was forced to flee west to the highlands. There the Khumalos attacked Tswana people, who were in turn forced to flee and to wage war on their neighbors. Over the next twenty years, the Matabele, as the Khumalos were later called, fought as they went until at last they set up a new kingdom in Bulawayo (now in Zimbabwe). Other defeated refugees traveled north to set up new kingdoms in the areas that are now Mozambique and Tanzania. Others went south along the coast, and so the fighting spread.[4]

The effect of these *Mfecane/Difagane* wars was to weaken many of the old political structures and to make them vulnerable at the very moment when Europeans arrived in the region looking for new lands to settle.

One Sotho chief, Moshoeshoe, built up a nation by a different method. He took his people to a flat-topped mountain east of the Caledon River. There they built an unconquerable fortress-capital. While Moshoeshoe was prepared to fight if need be, he was a flexible and conciliatory diplomat as well. To those who surrendered, he lent back their captured cattle in return for their loyalty and allegiance.[5]

Europeans settlers arrive in South Africa

Although Portuguese and English ships had explored the South African coasts in the sixteenth and seventeenth centuries, it was the Dutch East India Company which, in 1652, created the first settlement of Europeans at the Cape of Good Hope. The company needed a base from which to control entry into the Indian Ocean and to supply its ships with fresh water, meat and vegetables.

At first, the Khoi-Khoi herders of the Cape were glad to sell sheep and cattle to the Dutch. But soon the Dutch began to set up farms and ranches on the land that the Khoi-Khoi, the Khoi-San and their ancestors had used for centuries. In 1659 war broke out when the Dutch attacked the Khoi-Khoi and captured and imprisoned their leaders for sheltering slaves escaped from Dutch farms. Thus began a series of wars between the Khoi-Khoi and the Khoi-San peoples and the new settlers; the central issue was the encroachment of the Dutch on the Africans' traditional pasturage and hunting grounds.

"If we came to your country, would you allow us to do the same thing?" the Khoi-Khoi asked. But neither the Khoi-Khoi nor the other Khoi-San people were a military match for the Europeans. They lacked central political organization as well as horses and guns needed for an effective defense.[6]

The wars, however, did not kill nearly as many Africans as did the epidemics of smallpox, which spread from European ships from 1713 on. Deprived of land and livestock by war and decimated by disease, Khoi-San society fell apart.[7] By 1800 there remained only a tenth of the 200,000 Khoi-Khoi and Khoi-San estimated to have lived on the Cape a century earlier. Most of the Khoi-Khoi men chose to become herders for their conquerors, paid only in housing, food, brandy and tobacco. But slavery, not free labor for wages in cash or kind, was to be the foundation on which the Dutch colonists built their wealth. The Dutch East India Company imported slaves from West Africa, India, Malagasy or the East Indies for farm and household labor. From Europe the company recruited small farmers (*boers* in Dutch) to manage the land the company gave them. After 1688, French Huguenots fleeing persecution and German Lutherans joined the Dutch colonists and became part of their culture, already being reshaped by relocation. The Huguenots were assimilated into the Dutch Reformed Church, but the Lutherans retained their own religious identity.

Successful farmers grew rich from wheat grown in the black soil of Swartland and wines produced on the hillsides of Paarl and Stellenbosch. Company officials often enriched themselves through company monopolies of land and trade.[8]

The European settlers did not at first regard Africans as racially inferior. Rather, the initial prejudice against them was based on culture; Africans were regarded as uncivilized, savage, heathen and bestial.[9] Only when Africans began to adopt European customs, culture and religion were they rejected because of their race and color. The belief in racial inferiority that developed helped Europeans to rationalize more comfortably their conquest of the land—then they need not share their new wealth or their political rights with the more numerous Africans.

Europeans did not, by and large, marry outside their own race. But some African and other non-European women did accept European men as lovers or unofficial husbands; women who were slaves may not have had much choice. One in ten European men had a non-European woman as a lover or as a polygamous wife in addition to a European wife.

A European father could emancipate his children born to a mother who was a slave, but usually did not do so. Girls were sometimes freed, because they could not inherit property in any event.[10] Boys became privileged household servants or even overseers. Soon Cape Town developed a small free, "Coloured" community. Many of these freed persons retained the Malay culture and Muslim religion which they or their relatives had brought from Asia when they were imported as slaves. They became artisans and craftspeople. On the frontier at the edge of the area settled by Europeans, the Khoi-San strain was dominant in this growing mixed-race group. Some migrated north, joining with Khoi-San people and becoming the Orlam and Griqua peoples.

The "Coloured" population of South Africa today, which is located primarily in the Cape province and numbers two and a half million, originated in this interbreeding of European settlers and sailors, Asian and African slaves, and the Khoi-San. Many accepted as "white" in South Africa today, perhaps as many as 10 percent, have unacknowledged African or Asian ancestors.

The Trekboers

Because of the slavery system, young and landless Europeans did not take farm labor jobs. Many became *trekboers* instead. Pushing east and north, these frontiersmen traded with the Khoi-San or hunted game. Settling on a new piece of "company" land, they would stake out a farm of 6,000 acres or more. The Africans already living there found themselves treated as "squatters" on land which they considered theirs. Young African men might become "apprentices" (that is, temporary slaves). Others were forced to migrate or take up resistance to the invaders.

To the north in the semi-desert region of Karoo, Khoi-San resisters using bows and arrows pushed the trekboers back south in the 1770s and again in the 1790s. But they fought for a losing cause; trekboer *commando*[*] squads, armed with rifles and mounted on horses, hunted down the Khoi-San. In the grasslands of the Suurveld to the east, from 1779 to 1812 the trekboers fought four inconclusive wars over cattle and land with the Xhosa clan.

Some trekboers adopted the culture of the Africans, living beyond the frontier in wagons or reed and thatch houses. Their sheep, the kind kept by the Khoi-San, came to be called *Afrikaner* sheep. They copied traditional African food and clothing. They spoke *Taal*, which borrowed words and phrases from the

---

[*] This was the first use of "commando," which entered English vocabulary from Afrikaans, as did "trek."

Portuguese, Malay, Khoi-San and Bantu languages and grafted them onto a Dutch root stock, thus creating a dialect called *Afrikaans*. Culturally and economically, the *Afrikaners*, as these pioneers came to be called, were not very different from the Africans among whom they lived.[11] Eventually, almost all the descendants of the original Dutch, French and German settlers spoke this dialect and called themselves Afrikaners.

The British take over the Cape

In 1795 the British Empire seized the Cape in order to protect the sea passage that Britain saw as strategic in its war with France. After a brief restoration of Dutch rule, the British occupied the Cape again in 1806 and began to develop it as a colony. To reduce the cost of garrisoning troops, they settled veterans of the wars with France along with their families on the eastern frontier.

The British soon alienated the Afrikaner settlers by liberalizing the colonial system. They intended to build up a capitalist form of farming using free labor rather than slaves. (As we shall see in the next chapter, British missionaries helped bring about this change.) Vagrancy and apprenticeship laws, which had forced Khoi-San people to work for Boer or English masters, were repealed. Better wages rather than force were to lure workers to farms. Africans began to have legal rights.

The English also decreed that the cost of frontier wars with African societies was to be borne by the Boer settlers. More disturbing yet to the Boers was the abolition of their system of local, democratically elected court officers in favor of a centralized system of law, administered by resident magistrates and commissioners. English was declared the language of the courts and of most schools.[12]

Although these were important causes of resentment among the Boers, more significant was Britain's decision in 1833 to abolish slavery gradually throughout its Empire. Soon thereafter, a large part of the Afrikaner population with their servants and slaves began the Great Trek (migration), heading north to find land beyond British control. The Trek was a key event in forming the Afrikaners' identity as a nation. The pioneer spirit of these *Voortrekkers* is today celebrated in story, legend and myth, especially by conservative Afrikaners. Although the Voortrekkers called themselves patriots and voiced anti-imperial slogans similar to those of the American revolutionaries of fifty years earlier, the

Boer revolt against British rule was largely untouched by the human rights philosophy of the Enlightenment—the philosophy that led the framers of the U.S. Constitution to debate but not abolish slavery. What Afrikaners wanted was democracy for themselve and a free hand in dealing with Africans.[13]

The Great Trek

Crossing the Orange River into the land of the Tswana and the Sotho, the trekker wagon trains at first were welcomed by some of the African kings, since hospitality to those in distress is an African tradition. Believing the trekkers' stay would be temporary, Moshoeshoe, chief of a Sotho clan, and other chiefs allowed them use of land. Soon, however, the Boers claimed the land as their own and wars over cattle began.

Crossing the Vaal River to the north, trekker hunters entered the territory controlled by Mzilikazi of the Matabele (see page 21). Mzilikazi attacked the trekkers for poaching game and captured their livestock. The Boer trekkers, strengthened by new arrivals led by Piet Retief, a rich and politically active slaveholder, retaliated: in November 1837, 300 mounted Boers, assisted by 50 Tswana warriors, routed the Matabele and drove them north across the Limpopo river.[14]

Meanwhile, Piet Retief was also negotiating for land with King Dingane, who had seized power from his brother Shaka (who had built up the Zulu nation into a strong military power). Dingane suspected the Boers of having stolen cattle from him. Retief defended himself by offering to get back the cattle, which in fact had been stolen by a Sotho chief. When Retief returned with some of the cattle, Dingane remained suspicious. Imagining treachery, he executed Retief, his soldiers and his servants. Then Dingane attacked the Boer camp at dawn, killing 500 people. In April 1838 a Zulu army defeated a Boer commando unit, which then retreated to land the settlers had already claimed on the highveld, the high plateau to the west.[15]

The Battle of Blood River—the Day of the Covenant

In November, Andries Pretorius, a rich Cape farmer, arrived with reinforcements. He called the Boer commandos to a "holy war" against the "heathen savage" Zulus. According to Afrikaner legend, the Boers vowed to keep forever holy the day on which God granted them a victory. In December a Zulu army attacked a Boer encampment on the Ncone River, which had been heavily protected by banks and ditches. Boer gunfire trapped the Zulus in the ditches and 3,000 Zulus were killed. Not a single Boer died. December 16, the Day of the Vow, is now a national day of thanksgiving in South Africa, a day when Afrikaners celebrate the anniversary of this massacre at "Blood River."

Six thousand Boers eventually moved into the eastern coast area of Natal and in 1839 set up the Natal Republic, with a *volksraad* (government assembly) at Pietermaritzburg. Each trekker family laid out farms of 6,000 acres or more. The claims of native Africans were ignored. Every African had to carry a pass in Boer territory on pain of being handed over to some Boer farmer who needed workers. Africans not working for Boer farmers were expelled into "native reserves."[16]

In 1843 the Natal Republic collapsed after the Boers unsuccessfully attacked the British settlement of Durban. Under British control the colony of Natal set up a strict policy of segregation much like that of the Boers. Africans were to be kept in reserves, their chiefs responsible to the British Lieutenant Governor. They were to use customary tribal law under white magistrates. Africans could not enter white towns except under strict influx controls. Instead, they were encouraged to work on farms and sugar plantations. Although "qualified" Africans were allowed to become voters, only a handful were able to do so.

On the Cape, there was a more liberal "qualified franchise," but it was short-lived. In 1853 the British-controlled Cape Colony allowed non-Europeans the right to vote—if one were an adult male, earned a certain income or owned a house of specified value. At first only a small number qualified, but some thirty years later non-European voters had become a majority in some districts. At that point, the qualifications were stiffened to make sure that whites alone ruled. The Cape "liberal franchise" finally was terminated in 1936.[17]

So although British liberalism was an advance over the slaveholding system of the Dutch, it shared with the Boers the fundamental principle of white supremacy and rule.

Until 1867 South Africa comprised a patchwork of African and European-descent societies living side by side; European conquest of the African societies was not complete. The Zulu kingdom and its army were still powerful. Moshoeshoe's kingdom of the Sotho people had never been subdued. British conflict with Boers had been resolved in the 1850s when the British acknowledged the independence of two Boer Republics organized in the northern highveld, the Orange Free State and the South African Republic. Traditional African societies, British colonies and Boer republics traded with one another and profited from the commerce.

The mineral revolution

The 1867 discovery of diamonds at Kimberly and the discovery of gold twenty years later in Johannesburg transformed the British Empire's interest in South Africa. This land was no longer an expensive strategic outpost with troublesome "native vs. settler" conflicts; it became a treasured source of wealth. The conquest of the entire land was now worth completing. The British first conquered and subdued the remaining African societies, ending in the Zulu War of 1878-79, and then the Boer states in 1899-1902.

The diamond discoveries brought diggers, prospectors, traders, saloon-keepers and missionaries to the region. Boer farmers uprooted their families in search of new wealth but often ended up as "poor whites," unable to cope with the ruthless, wily immigrants who outwitted and dominated them. Unskilled and uneducated, Afrikaners often found work as overseers of black laborers, earning six times as much as the African workers. Africans moved into the prospecting region in search of the price of a rifle, and later, of European clothes and liquor.

The 1886 discovery of gold proved even more important than diamonds in the transformation of South Africa. As word spread about the huge gold deposits in the Witwatersrand* area of the Transvaal, a mining boom mushroomed on a scale that made the California gold rush of the 1840s seem small-time. Griqua claims to the land were denied and legally abolished. Some who had been able to make fortunes by investing in diamond mining were now prepared to invest in gold mining. John Hays Hammond and other American mining engineers earned princely sums for advising these "Rand Lords," mining capitalists primarily of British and German origin, who had become economic barons of the Witwatersrand. Hammond persuaded U.S. foreign policy makers that the minerals of South Africa were of strategic importance.

---

* *Witwatersrand* literally means White Waters' Reef. The Rand is a geological structure some 25,000 feet thick which contains veins or reefs bearing gold ore. It is the world's largest gold field, extending over 100 miles at its widest point with its center at Johannesburg. A Rand is the South African unit of currency.

Entrepreneurs from many countries, especially Britain and Germany, invested in complex machinery; they imported European miners needed to do the skilled work. Although the Afrikaners outnumbered the British and other Europeans in South Africa, the mining industry was almost entirely controlled by British and German financiers. Conflicts soon developed between these Rand Lords who owned the mines and the Boer Republics in which the mines were situated. The businessmen alleged that the Transvaal government was corrupt. They were especially concerned that the government could not deliver a regular supply of cheap, submissive labor. Moreover, as *Uitlanders* (foreigners), they had no vote in the Boer Republics.

Gold starts a war

John Cecil Rhodes, the leading Rand Lord, had the ear of London policy makers. Rhodes was the principal figure in the De Beers diamond monopoly and also in Consolidated Gold Fields. He had organized the British South Africa Company, which had taken over the land of the Matabele, Shona and other African people to the north. It was this company that, beginning in 1891, ran "Rhodesia" as a private British-chartered corporation. Rhodes was also prime minister of the Cape Colony. Angered by the limits that Boer control of the mining areas put on mining profitability and possible British expansion, in 1895 he plotted with his administrator in Rhodesia to raid Johannesburg in hopes of starting a revolt against the Boer Republics. Even though the raid failed, Rhodes never lost sight of his prime objective: a British Africa stretching from "Cape to Cairo."

In 1899 Rhodes and other British businessmen in South Africa persuaded London to intervene to secure their interests and the Anglo-Boer war broke out. Nearly half a million British troops were sent to fight one-tenth as many Afrikaner soldiers. The Empire poured millions of pounds into the war, using brutal scorched-earth tactics in order to take over all South Africa. British forces burned Boer homes and farms and confined many Afrikaner civilians in concentration camps, where over 20,000 people died—most of them women and children—from malnutrition and disease.

The 1902 peace treaty of Vereeniging ended the war and secured British mining interests, although Afrikaners would be the majority of the voting population.[18]

The Union of South Africa

After the war, white South Africans sought national unity. Britain was anxious to avoid further costly conflict with the Afrikaners. The solution seemed to lie in granting self-government and dominion status to a union or federation of the Transvaal and the Orange Free State (the Afrikaner republics) with the two English-speaking colonies, Natal and the Cape. Each was to become a province in the Union of South Africa. At a national convention in 1908, delegates from each region agreed on a draft consititution, which set forth a union form of government. The Convention tried to mollify the various white political factions by geographic compromises: the Cape would be the seat of the new two-chamber Parliament; the Transvaal, which was the economic center, would get the government's administrative center in Pretoria, a town north of Johannesburg; and Bloemfontein in the Orange Free State would be the judicial capital.

The whites refused any expanded political role for blacks, for whom the Union proved a net loss. Transvaal, Natal, and the Orange Free State refused to make the Cape franchise into a national right for all people. Instead, each province would be free to decide the suffrage question as it saw fit. In addition, the Convention ruled that only whites could sit in Parliament—this had been the practice on the Cape but had never been law. Africans, "Coloured" people and "Indians" expressed their outrage and disapproval politely but firmly. They condemned the "colour bar" publicly and sent delegations to Britain—in vain. Britain had no intention of upsetting the carefully crafted compromise arrangement or the white settlers who had crafted it by intervening. Britain reserved for itself only decisions concerning war and peace.

In May 1910 a South African Union government came into existence. Dedicated to conciliating Boers and Britons, it was headed by an Afrikaner general, Louis Botha. All subsequent administrations continued to be headed by Afrikaners. Another Afrikaner general became the most famous symbol of Afrikaner loyalty to the British Empire. Jan Smuts was almost as well known as Winston Churchill as an Empire statesman. It was Smuts who led South African troops in the conquest of German Southwest Africa (now Namibia), directed a campaign aginst the Germans in East Africa and became a prominent member of the British war cabinet in World War I. Later, Smuts served as Prime Minister of Union governments from 1919-1924 and 1939-1946. He was a signer of

the United Nations Charter. Yet in spite of his image as a wise
and liberal statesman, Smuts believed that the future of Africa
lay with whites of British and Dutch descent, not with blacks:
"If left to themselves, [Africans] do not respond very well to the
stimulus of progress." Whites would have to civilize the "natives."[19]

Gold creates a labor force

With the end of the Anglo-Boer war, gold mining resumed in
earnest, along with the search for ways to accumulate capital and
recruit labor in order to maximize profits. The gold fields may
have been the world's largest discovered to date, but the ore was
low-grade, deep and scattered. To produce one ounce of gold,
four tons of rock had to be extracted and processed. The price
of imported machinery, equipment and supplies kept going up,
while the price of gold was usually fixed on the fluctuating
international market.

The mine owners needed solutions to two problems: how to
centralize capital in order to direct it efficiently and accumulate
it rapidly; and how to obtain cheap, abundant labor that could
be easily controlled.

To accomplish the first objective, powerful owners consolidated
the mines under financial holding companies. By 1910 all mines
had been gathered under an umbrella of six great mining "houses."
These monopolies combined to form a Chamber of Mines that
set labor policies, wages and other standards, becoming the driving
force behind the policies of the South African government.

To accomplish the second objective of a cheap labor supply,
the government required Africans to pay taxes on their land and
houses, thus compelling black people who were living at a
subsistence level to enter the labor market to get cash wages.
Thus the Africans' new need for money eased the task of the mine
labor recruiters. In order to control the workers, mine owners used
a compound system: African mine workers, who were not allowed
to bring families with them, were crowded into all-male dor-
mitories. Workers from different tribes were kept separated and
under close guard to make organizing strikes or protests difficult.

To keep wages down, the Chamber of Mines monopolized all
recruiting of labor and set uniform wages at levels that remained
low until the 1970s. By setting up this system that depended on
migrant black labor, the mine owners did not have to pay for
the upkeep of workers' families. Instead, laborers visited their

families only for a week or two each year. In most systems of actual slavery as practiced earlier in South Africa, in the Americas and elsewhere, the slaveholder also had the upkeep of a slave's family. In the mines, where black workers were highly controlled although not technically slaves, the mine owners left the burden of feeding the workers' dependents with the families themselves, who scratched out an existence in barren "native" reserves.

When Africans did not respond to the wages and conditions in the mines in sufficient numbers, workers from China were imported and indentured until, after ten years, the British Parliament stopped such an obvious form of servitude. Later, migrants from Mozambique, Lesotho, Botswana, Rhodesia and elsewhere were recruited to take many of the dirty, dangerous, low-paying jobs.

To get the skilled labor necessary for deep mining, the owners imported miners from Europe and America. Because their pay depended on the amount of ore mined, these highly paid white workers tended to pressure Africans in their charge to produce. They organized militant trade unions to protect their interests against the mine owners, but they did not include Africans in their organizing efforts. Instead, they demanded and got "job colour bars" (which eventually became national law) in order to keep the good jobs for themselves.[20]

Agriculture

At the turn of this century, African peasant farmers were expanding their own farms and competing successfully with whites for the new markets created by mining. Africans bought land from whites or became sharecroppers on white-owned land. In addition, many Africans went to the mines in preference to working at lower wages on white farms.

Eventually, white farmers found themselves short of labor. Instead of raising wages to attract labor, white farmers lobbied for and got the 1913 Natives Land Act, which prevented Africans from buying or squatting on white-owned land. Africans could now own land in only 7 percent of the country; thousands were forced to give up their own farming and hire themselves out at low wages or migrate to "native reserves."

In the province of Natal, another solution to the farm labor shortage was adopted. From 1860 on, sugar plantation owners imported indentured servants from India to work their cane fields.

By the end of the century, the number of Indians in Natal had reached 100,000. Many eventually became landowners; some became merchants or professionals. The threat of their rising power and wealth led to an anti-Indian campaign. In 1896, Natal took away Indian voting rights, imposed poll taxes and restricted trading licenses.[21]

Industrial production

Mining development led in turn to development of industries to serve the needs of the new wage-earners and consumers as well as the industrial needs of mines. Shortages created by World War I stimulated the rapid growth of local manufacturing. As in the mines, the skilled work force was white; the unskilled workers were migrant African men who left their families in areas reserved for "natives" or in Botswana, Mozambique and other nearby countries that began to supply more of the mine labor.

In 1924 a new national administration pledged to develop local industry came to power. It set up a state-owned iron and steel industry and imposed tariffs to protect the manufacturing industries, which tended to be small. Equally important, the government set up a national system of collective bargaining and wage-setting that favored mechanized production. More and more African workers entered the manufacturing sector, but they were excluded from the collective bargaining that set their wages. By 1939, 800,000 Africans worked in mining and manufacturing.

The state continued to maintain a system of "influx control" under which blacks were admitted to cities only to "minister to the needs" of whites. When blacks were no longer employed, they were to leave and return to their "native" areas.

The Afrikaners are left out

The Afrikaners were not entrepreneurs or investors except in agriculture, a sector now representing a much smaller percentage of the national product than mining and manufacturing. Discriminated against in industry by owners in favor of English-speaking or imported European workers, Afrikaners held the worst positions in the white job market. Many were employed as unskilled laborers, railway workers, mine workers and bricklayers. They felt especially threatened by the influx of African workers into industry, where blacks were beginning to find skilled and semi-skilled jobs. As African wages rose and African trade unions became more militant during World War II, Afrikaner workers felt their privileged niche in the white work force crumbling.

Their disadvantaged position provided fertile soil for a strong new racist and nationalist ideology. The Afrikaner republic of their dreams would throw off the "golden chains of British imperialism" and advance the interests of the *Volk* (the white Afrikaner nation) through state-controlled enterprises (parastatals) and by systematically and intensively exploiting black Africans.

The new ideology was called *apartheid* (pronounced apart-hate) or "separateness." Afrikaner theologians provided it with a theological rationale. Apartheid became a kind of "Christian" nationalism like that practiced in Germany under National Socialism. Many Afrikaner clergy were part of the Broederbond (Band of Brothers), a secret society of well-educated, articulate and powerful men, who were determined to preserve Afrikaner interests, unity and identity at all costs. The Broederbond strove to end British domination in thought, culture and politics and to defend South African white society against the "black threat."[22]

During World War II, some leaders of the Afrikaner Nationalist party, which was gaining membership and influence, supported the Fascist powers. In the newspaper he edited, Hendrik Verwoerd, later Prime Minister of South Africa, openly promoted the Nazi cause. Balthazar John Vorster, who became Prime Minister after Verwoerd, commanded a right-wing terrorist group and was jailed for his pro-Nazi activities.

World War II initiated a period of rapid economic growth in which more and more black South Africans became part of the wage-earning population. They organized strong trade unions, which were able to carry out successful strikes. Their real earnings rose by 50 percent from 1939 to 1948, and the gap between white and black wages began to close. The African National Congress (ANC), an organization founded in 1912 to promote African interests and unity, became more militant, demanding for the first time that all South Africans should have the right to vote. Its Youth League stressed new methods of mass resistance. The ANC declared that they wanted to see the Atlantic Charter, signed by Roosevelt and Churchill, implemented in South Africa. The Charter had recognized "the right of all people to choose the form of government under which they will live." In view of that declaration of Allied goals, many black soldiers who had fought with the official South African forces for the Allied cause in World War II asked why they should not enjoy the rights of democracy at home.[23]

The Nationalist Party comes to power

It was in this context that in 1948 the Afrikaner Nationalist Party came to power with a mandate to enforce the complete separation of the races in all spheres of life and to maintain and strengthen white supremacy. It was soon clear what the designers of apartheid meant by that term:

- A policy of "bleeding the black trade unions to death" attempted to reverse recent gains. Strikes were outlawed; workers could negotiate only through "works committees" under the bosses' control.
- Pass laws and influx control were intensified; segregation in all spheres would be strictly enforced.
- The Suppression of Communism Act was passed in 1950. Not only did it outlaw the Communist Party, it also allowed the Minister of Justice to restrict and ban anything he considered "communist activity." It was used to smash the black labor movement (in which the Communist Party of South Africa had been a significant force) and to break up anti-apartheid organizing activities, meetings and rallies.

Early opposition to apartheid

The apartheid program launched in 1949 was a severe blow to the black political and labor movements that had been struggling for a democratic South Africa. In response, the African National Congress adopted in 1949 a program of mass boycotts, strikes and civil disobedience. Although the planned program was peaceful and nonviolent, it met violent police repression. In May 1950 the police broke up a May Day demonstration with guns and clubs, killing eighteen black demonstrators. In 1952 the ANC launched the Defiance Campaign, in which thousands disobeyed the new laws—some so minor as using a toilet reserved for another race—in order to fill the jails so full that enforcing the law would become impossible. Thousands, black and white, were jailed.

The government broke the campaign by enacting tough new laws: civil disobedience could lead to heavy fines, confiscation of one's property, imprisonment for up to ten years or ten strokes of the lash. But the Defiance Campaign had a number of positive results.[24] The ANC grew tenfold to over 100,000 members and succeeded in drawing together a network of groups ready for closer cooperation. An alliance was formed in 1954 between the ANC, the Indian Congress, the Coloured People's Congress and the Congress of Democrats (a small group of anti-racist whites). Together they planned a "Congress of the People" that would envision the democratic society for which the groups were striving.

On June 26, 1955, several thousand delegates from the Congress alliance met in Kliptown, near Johannesburg. At this historic meeting they adopted the Freedom Charter, which stills stands today as the single most important statement of the position of the ANC and other anti-apartheid groups. Based on the United Nations Declaration of Human Rights, it calls for a democratic and non-racist state in which every man and woman shall have the right to vote and to stand for office, regardless of race, religion or sex. The Freedom Charter calls for equal rights to speak, meet, preach, worship, travel and get an education. To ensure democratic control of the economy, it calls for national ownership of the minerals, the banks and other monopolies for the benefit of all the people.[25] (For the Charter's text, see *Until We Are Free*.)

To the government, this document appeared revolutionary and utterly seditious. An ANC member who participated in the Congress recently recalled the passion with which the Congress had to defend the charter from police seizure:

> The racist army and police could not touch us, and moved off, sealing all entrances and leaving only one, where all three thousand delegates were searched and papers and Freedom Charters removed. One woman swallowed it rather than let the police get hold of it. A man put the Xhosa version in his socks. Babla Saloojee . . . jumped over the wall with his copy and was able to give it to the press. They were not successful in obliterating the charter. [From a Freedom Day speech made by an ANC participant, June 26, 1986]

The Treason Trial

Shortly after the Congress, the government launched a series of police and army raids to gather evidence of the revolution which it believed was being hatched. Then, late in 1956, police arrested 156 Congress participants and charged them with high treason.

The Treason Trial dragged on for four years. One of the defendants, a black lawyer named Nelson Mandela, emerged as principal spokesperson for all those on trial. Mandela insisted that the ANC had always been committed to nonviolence. He denied that he was a Communist and that the ANC was a Communist organization, although it had some Communist members; the ANC was a broad-based alliance of those opposed to white supremacy. When one justice asked Mandela, "Well, as a matter of fact, isn't your freedom a threat to Europeans*?" Mandela replied:

> No, it is not a direct threat to the Europeans. We are not anti-white, we are against White supremacy and in struggling against White supremacy we have the support of some sectors of the European population. . . . It is quite clear that the Congress has consistently preached a policy of race harmony and we have condemned racialism by whomever it is professed.[26]

Finally the judges (all of them white) threw out the government's case: "On the evidence presented, it is impossible for this court to come to the conclusion that the ANC has acquired or adopted a policy to overthrow the state by violence."[27]

While the trial was going on, the government changed its laws to fit whatever accusations it might choose to make. From then on, the governent could ban any organization it saw fit to label communist, subversive or "unlawful," and no court could interfere. Evidence became irrelevant.

Meanwhile, the trade union movement grew stronger. The newly formed South African Congress of Trade Unions (SACTU) fought plans to "bleed the unions to death." Women often led the trade union movement, especially in such industries as food and clothing, where women workers predominated. Women, black and white, also vigorously campaigned against the extension of pass laws.

The Sharpeville Massacre

By the late 1950s, a split had developed in the African National Congress. A group of young militants, who called themselves "Africanists," argued that ANC should not work closely with whites. They contended that a society that stacks the deck of privilege and power in favor of whites makes it almost impossible for whites to work with blacks without taking charge. Robert Sobukwe, the Africanists' leader, was against driving whites out of the country: a black "pigmentocracy" would not be better than

---

* A term used for white South Africans into the 1960s.

a white one. But whites and Indians must drop their arrogant assertions of superiority and give their primary loyalty to Africa.

In April 1959 these Africanists broke from the ANC and formed the Pan Africanist Congress of Azania*(PAC), which called for a more confrontational strategy, refusing to rule out the use of violence.

In early 1960, the PAC planned a nationwide anti-passbook campaign. On March 21, at Sharpeville, an African township in the Transvaal, Sobukwe led 10,000 people to the police station. Most had no passbooks and many were seeking to be arrested. The slogan of their nonviolent resistance was "No bail, no defense, no fine!" The crowd was noisy but not hostile. Then, at point-blank range, the police opened fire. People fled in panic, while the police continued firing into the backs of the running crowd. When the firing stopped, 40 women, 21 men and 8 children lay dead; 180 were injured.

Black anger erupted in mass boycotts of work. The army forced many people to go to work at gunpoint. The police arrested thousands of Africans, including Sobukwe and other PAC leaders, and banned the PAC and ANC under the new Unlawful Organizations Act passed just after the Sharpeville massacre.[28]

The Sharpeville massacre, which made the violence of the apartheid regime fully visible to the world, became a critical turning point in South African history. International voices demanded sanctions against the Nationalist government.

After the massacre, the ANC and PAC changed their tactics and decided that nonviolent protest was no longer enough to confront a government prepared to use ruthless force against peaceful demonstrations. For half a century black Africans had used only peaceful means of struggle, but these means had not brought conversion, enlightenment or transformation. They certainly had not altered the violently unjust power structure. Indeed, the fruit of nonviolent protest lay on the ground at Sharpeville. Armed defense, even armed offense, seemed a necessary next step.

In 1961-62, therefore, the ANC formed an underground army called *Umkhonto we Sizwe* (the Spear of the Nation), which launched a sabotage campaign against structures like power lines yet avoided causing harm to people. The PAC also formed a small army, which

---

* Azania is the name given to the east coast of Africa by a Greek shipping guide in the second century A.D. The root is from the Persian *Zanji-bar*, meaning "the coast of black people." Some Africans now use Azania as their name for South Africa.

carried out a few assassinations of police and informers. These efforts, which were quite amateurish at this stage, foundered. PAC militants fled or were swept up by the police. ANC's underground army was betrayed by informers; its headquarters were raided and its leadership arrested. Nelson Mandela, on trial for his life in 1964, once again stated the case against apartheid:

> The complaint of Africans is not that they are poor and the Whites are rich, but that the laws which are made by the Whites are designed to preserve this situation.
> Above all we want equal political rights, because without them our liabilities will be permanent. I know this sounds revolutionary to the Whites in this country, because the majority of voters will be Africans. This makes the [Whites] fear democracy.[29]

Nelson Mandela and seven other ANC leaders were sentenced to life imprisonment.

The aftermath of Sharpeville

The 1960 mass killing at Sharpeville riveted world attention on South Africa as never before. Sharpeville became synonymous with ruthless, tyrannical racism. Virtually every member of the United Nations condemned the massacre and agreed to place a voluntary embargo on arms sales to South Africa. The World Council of Churches convened a conference in South Africa to consider the implications of Sharpeville for the church. In the same period, South Africa declared itself a Republic outside the British Commonwealth, further isolating itself from international influence and pressure.

These events also had a profound impact on foreign investors in South Africa. From 1959 through 1964, South Africa lost a net total of half a billion Rands (then about $700 million) in capital funds to other markets.[30]

Yet the "Sharpeville Crisis" did slowly subside. A brilliant generation of resistance leadership had been jailed or forced into exile. The South African government won the aid of international banks in restoring investor confidence. Chase Manhattan and Citicorp were among U.S. banks that advanced loans to show their confidence in South Africa's future. Although it had withdrawn from the British Commonwealth in 1961, South Africa was not without friends in the international investment world.

A decade (1963-73) of uninterrupted prosperity followed. British, American and other foreign investors poured in new money. For the first time, Afrikaner businessmen began to take part in capitalist mining and manufacturing enterprises. It was a period of apparent stability but not of peace. The forces of resistance to apartheid were rebuilding and would soon break forth again. Inspired by the 1974 collapse of the Portuguese colonial system, a whole new generation of militant activists was arising.

The Soweto uprising

On June 16, 1976, in Soweto, an African township outside Johannesburg, and elsewhere in the country, young secondary school students rose up in protest against the inferior "Bantu"[*] school system and against the apartheid that designed it. Over 600 died when police opened fire on angry, stone-throwing youths. Thousands went into exile, some to study and some to take up training for guerilla warfare. The stuggle had not died: it had continued and was now moving ahead more intensely than ever and with greater mass support.

Winnie Mandela, an anti-apartheid leader and the wife of Nelson Mandela, speaks directly to the heart of the revolt:

> As I have told the South African public time and time again, race relations in this country have deteriorated to the extent that there will no longer be any possible reconciliation between black and white. What is happening is, in fact, a projection of black anger against the racist regime. This anger is directed at anything that is connected with the system and the government. It is not a question of the insistence on the Afrikaans language as the mode of instruction for black schoolchildren. . . . It has got nothing to do with vandalism . . . it is black anger against white domination.[31]

---

[*] At this time, the government used the term "Bantu" for Africans of any ethnic group. "Bantu" education, initiated in 1955, limited the amount and quality of education for Africans, so that they could not become skilled in subjects needed for good jobs. Instruction in primary schools was to be carried out in the various African "mother tongues" or languages. English was to be the medium of instruction only in secondary schools. What the students of Soweto and elsewhere were objecting to specifically was the order to teach arithmetic, mathematics, social studies and one-half of all classes in Afrikaans, a language few teachers were proficient in. See Baruch Hirson, *Year of Fire, Year of Ash*, pp. 40-47, 59-60, 99-100.

Chapter Three:

The Church Struggles For Its Soul

No one, however thoroughly he enquired, has ever been able to find among all the Kaffirs or Hottentots or Beachrangers any trace of religion or any show of honour to God or the Devil. [Olfert Dapper, a seventeenth-century ethnographer]

Astonishing as Dapper's judgment must seem to us today, it was by no means unusual among Europeans of his time. The first Christians who came to the Cape Colony brought with them not only their own church, the Dutch Reformed Church, but also the prevailing prejudices of their time.

Anthropologists today confirm what Africans have always known about their own religious beliefs. As Archibishop Desmond Tutu points out, "We have always been a deeply religious people. This was so long before the advent of Christianity, and the African world view is at many points more consistent with the biblical world view than that emanating from the West."[1]

At the time Christians first arrived in South Africa, Africans believed in God as the Supreme Being, a transcendent Creator. The Sotho and Tswana people called God "Light," "Protector" and "Father." So sacred was God's name that the mere mention of it might cause death. Does this sound familiar? The Hebrew people also dreaded to say the name "Yahweh."

God was known as the creator of souls, the giver of breath and the God of destinies. Because Africans were so dependent on nature, they also believed in powers and spirits at work through all of nature, bringing good and evil, peace and war, health and disease, rain and drought. The spirits of the clan ancestors were mediators with the spirit world. As Mediterranean people did in New Testament times, Africans consulted mediums and healers in order to be in touch with the spirit world. (Recall that a large part of Christ's ministry involved casting out evil spirits or demons.) A wise king was sometimes seen as the embodiment of God's will, just as David was honored as God's anointed, one specially called and chosen.[2]

Early European settlers drew quick conclusions about African religion from scanty evidence. They saw Africans' reticence to talk about God as evidence that they had no God. Their belief in spirits was interpreted to be idolatry.

Although the Dutch saw Africans as religionless people, and the colony's two or three resident clergy felt the tug of mission, evangelizing the Khoi-Khoi would have meant learning a difficult language and perhaps living among them. The Reformed clergy had their hands full taking care of Europeans; converting Africans was not a high priority.[3] During the Cape Colony's first sixty years virtually no Khoi-Khoi were converted to Christianity. Until 1713 only one African had been baptized, a woman named Eva who married a Danish settler.

The missionaries arrive

It was not until the beginning of the modern missionary movement in the late eighteenth century that serious attempts were made to preach the gospel to Africans. The earliest missionaries were German Moravians, but the London Missionary Society (LMS), formed in 1795, sent most of the missionaries to southern Africa in the first half of the nineteenth century. The society was non-denominational but drew most of its funds and personnel from British Congregationalists. The mission movement grew as part of a revival of evangelical Christianity that emphasized the saving of individual souls, wherever they might be. Missionary fervor also intertwined with the expanding British Empire and its commercial, investment and political interests.

The most famous LMS missionary was John Philip, superinten-dent of the Society's work on the Cape from 1819 to 1851. Philip was a liberal of his day; that is, he believed that free-market forces bring inevitable progress. (Today this economic philosophy would be called conservative.) He argued against anti-vagrancy and passbook laws because they forced Africans into slavery or its equivalent. He lobbied the British government to substitute a free-labor wage system for slavery. Philip and his allies succeeded, and the new English settlers drew Africans into better-paid employment than the Boer farms offered. Philip also persuaded Britain to establish a system of friendship treaties with African chiefdoms in order to avoid wars on the frontier.

This liberalism of Philip and other missionaries did not appeal to the Boers, who saw them as troublemakers. But English settlers and the clergy who served them were scarcely more supportive when the missionaries tried to protect African rights. They tended to view the missionaries as traitors.

Some missionaries became powerful patriarchs among the Africans. William Anderson, LMS missionary from 1801 to 1820, set up a Griqua Republic with a constitution and coinage imported from Europe. Robert Moffat (1795-1883), who established a mission center at Kuruman, north of the Orange River, believed that the key to conversion was literacy. Africans, who had no written language, must learn how to read and write in their own tongue. So Moffat translated the Bible into Tswana. The Mfecane wars, however, led Moffat to conclude that Africans were hopeless and godless unless they were supervised and trained by European missionaries.

Appreciation—and separation

Missionaries of the Paris Mission took a different attitude in their work with the Sotho people. They idealized Moshoeshoe, the Sotho king, as a "noble savage," who revealed a Christian spirit in his efforts to achieve peace by negotiation with Europeans. And Moshoeshoe found these missionaries indispensable to his understanding of European intentions, technology and way of life.

Moffat's son-in-law was David Livingstone, who had a greater fame as a missionary. Livingstone also respected African culture and looked forward to independent, Christian African nations.

As Europeans penetrated the continental interior, Africans grew to depend on the advice of missionaries, who often used these opportunities to further imperial expansion. John Moffat, for example, used his father's influence with Mzilikazi, the Matabele king, to persuade his son, Lobengula, to open his lands to white usage and control. Such practices are why Africans say that when missionaries arrived, the Africans had the land and the missionaries had the Bible, but soon the Europeans had the land and the Africans had the Bible. Native Americans make a similar complaint.

While missionaries were almost inevitably agents of liberal imperialism, the message they brought should not be seen as captive to that ideology. Amid the devastating wars of the nineteenth century, the promises of the Christian faith made life bearable and dignified for many Africans. In time, the Word of

God was to become a powerful instrument of African liberation. Nevertheless, the nineteenth-century missionary message was often confused with the imperial domination and technological marvels that Europeans brought with them: better housing, lights, transportation, clothes.[4]

Furthermore, missions also became promoters of racial segregation. Most Protestant missionaries of that time felt that separate churches for settlers and Africans were necessary. They argued that, since Christianity seemed foreign to Africans, the church must become African to be accepted. While Anglican and Roman Catholic missionaries did not form separate denominational structures for Africans as the Protestants did, their settler congregations nevertheless were largely segregated from African congregations. Although these churches were multi-racial, racial discrimination and paternalism prevailed in most places.[5]

Dutch mission churches

The Dutch Reformed Church in South Africa gained its autonomy from the church in Holland in 1824 and established its own synod. In the mid-nineteenth century, this church also became caught up in the evangelical movement and began mission work among "Coloured" (mixed-race) people. Here, too, mission work led to segregation. In 1857 the Synod reversed its earlier stand that the Word of God called for communion to be served to all members "without destinction of colour or origin" (1829). Now, it decided, the "Heathen" must enjoy "Christian privileges" in separate buildings if whites objected to having communion with them. What was meant to be an exception soon became the rule. Separate congregations led to separate "mission" churches, such as the Nederduitse Gereformeerde Sendingkerk, established in 1881 for Coloured people; the Nederduitse Gereformeerde Kerk in Afrika organized for Africans, and the Indian Reformed Church.[6]

The practice of segregation in the Dutch Reformed Church was also influenced by attitudes of the Voortrekkers. Because these pioneers emigrated north in defiance not only of British colonial authorities but also of their own Synod, they went without clergy. The Voortrekkers took their family Bibles with them, read them avidly and interpreted them in their own way:

> As they journeyed, the pages came alive with meaning and relevance. The exodus of the people of Israel and their testing in the wilderness were happening again. Any obstacle along

the way to the promised land had to be overcome, by sheer grit and by the gun. Any doubt of divine providence was not only unthinkable, but blasphemy, a harbinger of disaster. The church at the Cape was no longer relevant, but the saga of Israel in the holy book was. [J.W. de Gruchy, *The Church Struggle in South Africa*, p. 20]

In 1853, the voortrekkers formed their own "Volkskerk" (people's church), formally called the Nederduitse Hervormde Kerk (NHK). Six years later, a further split took place. The new church that emerged, the Gereformeerde Kerk, reflected the more-Calvinist-than-Calvin views of a controversial Dutch theologian named Abraham Kuyper. Kuyper's ideas about separate and distinct spheres of politics, race and religion were enormously influential in shaping the thinking of all Afrikaner churches as they developed theories to justify racial segregation, later called apartheid.

Both of the new churches took a hard line on race: "No equality in church or state!" Today they continue as smaller, more extreme churches than the better-known Nederduitse Gereformeerde Kerk (NGK), the South African Dutch Reformed Church to which most Afrikaners belong. Yet their influence is disproportionately large because most Afrikaners want to keep their nation united in a common ideology.[7]

Prophetic voices: early forms of resistance

Today the vast majority of South African Christians are black. Their heritage is in the mission work, which was often and characteristically paternalistic, racially segregated and imperialistic, as we have seen. But most Africans have never accepted the notion of their own spiritual inferiority, even when they felt humiliated. On the contrary, a new generation of African Christians is urging the Christian churches of the world to join their struggle against racism and injustice. We in North America have much to learn from the vigor and strength of these Christians.

One way Africans resisted European domination of their religious culture was by forming independent African churches that combined Christian faith with traditional African religious practice. In South Africa today more than 3.5 million Africans belong to the 3,000 churches which make up the African Independent Churches Association (AICA). These churches vary in size from congregations of a handful to the 200,000 who belong to the Zion Christian Church. As recently as 1960s, mainline churches tended to view these independent churches as "nativistic" or pagan. Today they are increasingly recognized as a legitimate expression of resistance to the spiritually deadening influence of mission churches. As tribal societies crumbled and as more and more Africans experienced the numbing anonymity of urban life, the independent churches cushioned the impact of cultural change by drawing on the resources of the past to cope with new realities.

The independent churches choose to emphasize wholeness and healing amid disease and disintegration. While focussing on *cultural* resistance, they have remained as "apolitical" as possible and, in some cases, have been deferential to or supportive of apartheid political leaders. This position, as we shall see later, is now being challenged.[8]

For other Christians at the beginning of the twentieth century, resistance meant involvement in the politics of African nationalism. When the Union of South Africa was formed in 1910, black Christians took the lead in protesting segregation of the country and the church. They demanded that white Christians live up to their professed belief in the equality of all of God's children.

One such voice was that of Pixley ka Izaka Seme, born of Christian parents and a protege of the American Board Mission.* Educated at Columbia University and Oxford, Seme was typical of a new generation of African leaders. He initiated the first national conference of Africans in South Africa, held in 1912, which called for African unity, an end to tribal fighting and democratic rights for all South Africans. Out of this conference grew the organization that is today the African National Congress:

> Those who attended [the original conference] were the products of missionary education—ministers, teachers, clerks, interpreters, a few successful farmers, builders, small-scale traders, compound managers, estate and labour agents. . . . Like the followers of [Booker T.] Washington and [W.E.B.] Du Bois in the USA, they were setting out to attain what they considered their constitutional rights—equality of opportunity within the economic life and political institutions of the wider society. They believed Western and Christian

---

* The ABM was a mission, primarily in Natal, of the American Board of Commissioners for Foreign Missions, a non-denominational voluntary society supported by Congregationalists, Presbyterians and members of other Reformed churches. Seme was named Pixley in honor of an ABM missionary.

norms to be closely interrelated. . . . [P. Walshe, *The Rise of African Nationalism in South Africa*, p. 34]

The depth of white resistance to these comparatively modest demands compelled Africans to seek methods more effective than petitions and appeals to Christian values and to the alleged "civilized" and "democratic" ideals of Europeans, which turned out, in practice, to be for whites only. (We will hear details of this continuing search in Chapter Six.)

The English-speaking churches object to apartheid

It is important to remember that white resistance to African demands was not unbroken or unanimous. Within the English-speaking, basically white-dominated churches, voices were raised to protest at least some aspects of apartheid when it was introduced as government policy in 1948.

At an ecumenical conference in Rosettenville (a suburb of Johannesburg) in 1949, these churches—primarily those that belonged to the Christian Council of South Africa—called for unity through teamwork rather than apartheid. They called for extending the right to vote to all "capable of exercising it," for equal opportunity to the best education a community can provide and for the right to work according to one's ability. These demands sound modest in retrospect, displaying a certain air of paternalism; they were nonetheless an open and early opposition to apartheid.

While such resolutions criticized apartheid as a political theory, apartheid drew the strongest protest when it encroached upon the practices of church life. The Anglican and Roman Catholic churches both instituted and maintained important schools for African education; these schools received state subsidies. When the "Bantu" Education Act was adopted in 1953, the Anglican Church closed its schools rather than carry out the strict segregation the Act demanded. The Roman Catholic Church chose to keep their schools independent by assuming complete financial responsibility. When in 1957 the government proposed to give the Minister of Interior power to bar Africans from attending church in so-called "white" areas, even the cautious Anglican archbishop, Geoffrey Clayton, was stirred to accuse the state of trespassing on the church's freedom of worship. He told the authorities that his church would disobey the law. He was joined in this position by other English-speaking denominations, including the politically cautious Baptist Union.

Notwithstanding these actions and resolutions, modest as they were, the great majority of white churchgoers remained passive and uninvolved in the discussion and debate. In many cases, they neither sided with their own church leadership nor were critical of the government's apartheid policies.[9]

White prophets attack apartheid

It remained for certain prophetic white Christians to try to rouse the church from its torpor. For example, an Anglican priest, Michael Scott, took up the cause of Namibia, oppressed by South African occupation since 1915, and brought it to the United Nations. Scott was declared an undesirable immigrant and deported in 1950. An Afrikaner, B. B. Keet, a biblical scholar and theologian at the NGK seminary in Stellenbosch, demolished the argument for apartheid on biblical grounds in his 1955 book, *Whither South Africa?*

The most trenchant critique in the 1950s came from a missionary, Trevor Huddleston of the Community of the Resurrection, an Anglican religious order. Although Father Huddleston had taken part in the Congress of the People in 1955, the root of his protest against apartheid was not political. Rather, as a parish priest in the African township of Sophiatown, he had ministered to the suffering of Africans and celebrated the Eucharist with them. He had seen his parish literally bulldozed into oblivion to make room for a white suburb to be called Triomph (Triumph). Huddleston pled with Christians everywhere to understand the agony of Africans and to act against apartheid. In his book, *Naught for Your Comfort*, he caught the world's attention with a searing indictment of apartheid, ending on this note:

> . . . I do not know or trust the African: but I know and trust hundreds of Africans as my closest friends.
>
> You cannot love an abstraction: neither can you trust it; you can only know and love a person. It is the aim of the Government of South Africa to make it impossible for a white South African to know and to love a black South African. . . .
>
> In opposing the policies of the present Government, therefore, I am not prepared to concede that any momentary good which might conceivably emerge from them is good. . . . [or] that the motives which inspire such policies have any quality of goodness about them. For both the acts and the motives are inspired by a desire which is itself fundamentally evil and basically un-Christian: the desire to

dominate in order to preserve a position of racial superiority, and in that process of domination to destroy personal relationships, the foundation of love itself. That is anti-Christ. [T. Huddleston, *Naught for Your Comfort*, p. 182]

Shortly after his book was published, Huddleston was recalled to England by his order, although the order said it was supportive of him. (He later served as a bishop in two African countries, Tanzania and Malagasy, and then in East London.)

An equally controversial Anglican prophet held a greater position of authority in the church. Joost de Blank was born in the Netherlands and brought up as an evangelical Protestant. De Blank became an Anglican, then a priest, and in 1958, archbishop of Cape Town. While away from South Africa on a trip, he opened a highly critical attack on the churches' complicity with apartheid, singling out the Dutch Reformed churches for particular blame. After the Sharpeville massacre in 1960, he demanded that the World Council of Churches expel South Africa's Dutch Reformed churches from its membership. But de Blank's passionate, incisive criticism polarized opinion among Anglicans and alienated most white Christians in the country. Afrikaner Christians pointed out that Anglicans of South Africa were in no position to talk about racism when two-thirds of their clergy were white while two-thirds of their communicants were black. Other white Protestant church-people decried de Blank's authoritarian, acerbic manner even if they approved his ideas. Blacks, on the other hand, were delighted with his position and cheered him on.[10]

Christians respond to Sharpeville

As we have seen, for some Christians under apartheid the central question was: Is God calling us to disobey the laws of our nation when it calls itself Christian but sets itself above the gospel? Is it then an idol or, to use Huddleston's words, the anti-Christ?

A watershed in church thinking was the Cottesloe Conference of 1960, called by the South African member churches of the World Council of Churches in the aftermath of the Sharpeville massacre. The overwhelming majority of the delegates, including those from the NGK (the mainline Dutch Reformed Church), concluded that there was no justification in the Bible or theology for apartheid.

While this judgment sounds mild by today's standards, the South African government saw in it a challenge they were not prepared to ignore. Dutch Reformed Church theologians were told to get back into line. Hendrik Verwoerd, then Prime Minister, called on the NGK to keep a single mind on apartheid. As a result,

> Enough NGK theologians were tamed to ensure the continued support of apartheid. Some quietly withdrew from the political challenge of the day, others busied themselves with changing "individual attitudes," leaving the structural changes to others, and still others became the high priests of the Afrikaner civil religion that would justify apartheid .... There were a few—Beyers Naudé was one—who would eventually break their ties with the white NGK in order to be obedient to God. [Charles Villa-Vicencio, "An All-pervading Heresy,"in *Apartheid Is a Heresy*, p. 63]

The Cottlesloe Conference started Beyers Naudé on an extraordinary pilgrimage of faith, one that would make him well-known as a hero of faith throughout the churches of the world. Deeply rooted in Afrikaner culture and tradition, Naudé was a distinguished pastor of the NGK church, as his father had been. Not only was he the moderator of the NGK's Transvaal Synod, but he also was a long-time member of the secret Broederbond, the powerful society that shaped Afrikaner thought and action.

After Cottesloe, Naudé joined a small group of distinguished Afrikaners who refused to bow to the government's pressure. Instead, they signed a manifesto challenging the NGK and the government to reassess their position. In 1962 the group launched a magazine called *Pro Veritate* (On the Side of Truth) to publicize their position and to encourage discussion and debate.

The NGK saw the publication as subverting Afrikaner unity. Synods pushed their clergy to steer clear of Naudé and his colleagues. Naudé faced possible excommunication. In March 1963 he resigned from the Broederbond because he felt it was manipulating the church and destroying its freedom of conscience; after this, the break with his church was almost total.

The Christian Institute

In August 1963 Naudé became the director of a new ecumenical organization, the Christian Institute. Its purpose was to change Christians' awareness of and attitudes toward apartheid through programs of Bible study, prayer, reflection, social analysis and service. Reconciliation and unity could come through faith in God's purpose and Christ's redemptive action in overcoming barriers of history, culture, tradition, language and race.

Once again the NGK reacted with intense hostility. Naude's Synod gave him a stark choice: he must resign either his post as director of the Christian Institute or his status as a minister of the NGK. With anguish and pain Naudé chose the latter. In his last sermon to his congregation, he explained that it was a choice between "religious conviction and submission to ecclesiastical authority. By obeying the latter unconditionally I would save face but lose my soul." He saw his church crippled by fear, a "sign of unbelief," because it refused to face up to issues of racism and injustice, clinging to Afrikanerdom rather than to God's kingdom. His final words from the pulpit voiced his anguish:

> O my church, I call this morning in all sincerity from my soul—awake before it is too late. Stand up and give the hand of Christian brotherhood to all who stretch out the hand to you. There is still time, but the time is short, very short.

The Christian Institute was heavily influenced by the example of the Confessing Church in Hitler's Germany, in which theologians of the Reformed Church like Karl Barth and of the Lutheran Church like Dietrich Bonhoeffer had played an important roles. Dissenting Afrikaners of the Dutch Reformed tradition formed the core of the Institute, but their task was not confined to changing their own church. Led by Naudé, the Institute was to provide resources for and act as an avant-garde challenge to the smug complacency and lethargy of the white-dominated multi-racial churches.

Because it was not accountable to any church, the Institute was often free to act as a catalytic agent. In 1968 it joined with the South African Council of Churches[*] in a national consultation on Church and Society. The resulting "Message to the People of South Africa." clarified and strengthened the Cottesloe conclusions, declaring God's unshakable purpose to bring unity and salvation (wholeness) to the whole world. Apartheid was, on the contrary, a sinful policy in conflict with the Christian gospel.

The next year, the Christian Institute and the South African Council of Churches launched the Study Project on Christianity in Apartheid Society (SPROCAS). The goal was to move beyond the abstractions of the Message into practical ways of applying

---

[*] In 1968 the Christian Council changed its name to the South African Council of Churches. The Christian Council was organized in 1936; it included English-speaking and mission churches and, originally, the NGK (Dutch Reformed Church).

it, guided by a vision of a non-racial society reconciled through justice. By 1972 the Project's study phase was over. It had been led largely by white experts with only peripheral black participation. SPROCAS was critical of racism but inclined to trust in liberal capitalism and education as progressive forces capable of adequate reform. Many SPROCAS commissioners seemed fearful of losing white control and giving power to the poor; they did not fully recognize the necessity of black leadership and initiative.

The Institute under attack

The staff of the Christian Institute and of SPROCAS, however, were by this time ready for more radical conclusions. The final SPROCAS report, "A Taste of Power," recognized that South Africa was at a turning point. The white control model would not work. The initiative and power to change the society were passing into the hands of blacks.

An action program was initiated to follow up the new SPRO-CAS insights. A series of Black Community Programs meshed with the Black Consciousness movement already under way. Parallel efforts to raise white consciousness tended to disintegrate or turn toward traditional social welfare projects.

The Christian Institute saw its white membership shrink to a small but vital remnant, increasingly prepared let blacks take power and leadership. Financial support for Institute programs had dried up in South Africa; it depended almost entirely on help from churches overseas, especially those in the Netherlands.

The government, however, perceived the Institute as a powerful engine of evil; its endorsement of black power was clear evidence, if any was needed, of communist infiltration and influence. The government appointed a commission to investigate whether the Institute was putting foreign funds to subversive use. Naudé refused to cooperate in such a political witch hunt. As a result of the commission's findings, the Institute was declared an "Affected Organization:" it could no longer receive funds from overseas. Soon staff and projects had to be cut. Finally, in October 1977, after the death of Steve Biko, the best-known Black Consciousness leader, the government outlawed the Institute along with eighteen other anti-apartheid organizations, most of them black. Naudé himself was "banned"—restricted to his home for certain hours, allowed to see only one person at a time and not permitted to speak publicly or be quoted.[11]

The WCC funds liberation movements

The influence of churches outside South Africa, working in the World Council of Churches, also proved catalytic and controversial. Following its 1968 Assembly in Upsala, Sweden, where a major theme had been the churches' responsibility to deal with racism, the WCC Central Committee decided to launch a Programme to Combat Racism (PCR). When the member churches of the South African Council of Churches read the report of this decision, they were disturbed that the WCC seemed to accept that the use of force might be necessary to dislodge entrenched racism. Conversations with the WCC General Secretary, Eugene Carson Blake, still did not prepare them for the WCC's next step. In 1969 the WCC Central Committee adopted a PCR recommendation to make modest grants to the liberation movements of Southern Africa, including the African National Congress. The money was to be used exclusively for non-military purposes: education, organization and development work.

The multi-racial churches of South Africa were shocked and angered. The government was even more alarmed, considering this further evidence that the WCC had no interest in the gospel and was infiltrated by communist revolutionaries. The Dutch Reformed Church (NGK) joined in the hysteria. Prime Minister Vorster called for all South African churches to pull out of the WCC.

Finally, however, none of the WCC member churches of South Africa withdrew. They disassociated themselves from the grants decision and from any implication that violence was a legitimate means of Christian witness, but they refused to comply with Vorster's demand, pointing to apartheid's intrinsic violence. The conservative Presbyterian Church in South Africa, for example, refused to withdraw from the WCC, stating that while it dissented from guerilla violence, it dissented "at least as much from the violence inherent in the racial policies of the Government."[12]

The SACC endorses nonviolent resistance

As the Portuguese colonial system crumbled in 1974, socialist regimes came to power in neighboring Mozambique and Angola. White-ruled Rhodesia was increasingly threatened. These developments were greeted in South Africa with joy by blacks and with apprehension by the government. Fears of civil war increased as

Black Consciousness continued to rise. The churches' debate over the continuing WCC grants to the liberation movements began to be transformed by other considerations. If violence was wrong in principle, how could one defend the apartheid state's use of violence? If white Christians were conscripted for national service, should they consider refusing to participate?

In 1974 at Hammanskraal, near Pretoria, the South African Council of Churches answered Yes to this last question. It passed a resolution calling on its members to identify with the oppressed and to consider conscientious objection and passive resistance as nonviolent alternatives both to guerilla war and to state violence. The SACC declared that South Africa was a fundamentally unjust and discriminatory society, whose institutionalized violence had "provoked the counter-violence of the terrorist and freedom fighters." Thus it was hypocritical to deplore guerilla violence while preparing to defend South Africa with still more violence. If chaplains were to serve the armed forces at all, they should serve on both sides of the liberation struggle.

Reaction to the Hammanskraal Resolution demonstrated how polarized both the society and the churches had become. All the political parties, including the white opposition, condemned the resolution as undermining national security. The Cabinet and the NGK both called it treasonable. The government passed a law making encouragement of conscientious objection a serious crime. The member churches of the SACC, however, with varying enthusiasm did call on the government to respect conscientious objection and to provide alternatives to military service. The most vigorous support for the Hammanskraal resolution came from the Roman Catholic bishops. Black Christians—two-thirds of the Hammanskraal delegates were black—rejoiced that the church was at last moving to this kind of witness.[13]

Summing it up

As the Soweto crisis of 1976 approached, it became clear that new theologies were emerging within the church in South Africa, theologies of liberation similar to those of Latin America and of North American black theologians. In many quarters, theological and ecclesiastical leadership were now passing into black hands. White liberalism, its vitality exhausted, was no longer the source for solutions. Christians now had to take sides—either by joining the struggle for liberation or by opposing it.

Chapter Four:
A Society Divided Against Itself

South Africa has a planned economy. Its rulers have deliberately, purposefully divided it up in order to segregate Africans from people of European descent. By instituting a "homelands" policy that makes Africans into foreigners in their own country, apartheid aims to reduce them to political impotence. Their humanity is seen solely in their usefulness as cheap labor. Apartheid law also segregates and discriminates against others not of European origin: "Coloureds" and "Indians." This plan for segregation—sometimes called "separate development"—produces riches for some at the cost of poverty for most.

For most South Africans who are not of European origin, the wages of apartheid is poverty. This form of living death means poor health, high infant mortality, early death and inadequate education; it means poorly paid employment and vast unemployment in a land of great wealth and prosperity. Black women bear a special burden.

Having examined this society's development, including the church's involvement, it is now time to look more closely at what apartheid means. We begin with the experience of a woman who lives in one of the areas reserved by the authorities for blacks.

Things will only get worse

Rose is unemployed. She explains how life changed when the government started planning her rural area. They called it "betterment," which meant taking away her means of livelihood: the land and the cattle. It began in 1973, when the area where she lived was placed under the authority of a "homeland" chief.

Because of the planning system, the amount of land we have has decreased. Before planning, we could plough as much as we wanted. It is the agricultural department that plans. They have not worked with us.

We were staying outside this residential area and so we had to move when the [power] lines were cut. It was painful because the house I built was expensive and I got no compensation. But I had to oblige. We also had to get rid of our cattle because the planning system did not want them. . . .

Now we have no ploughing fields. We are dying of hunger. Once the agricultural officers called us together to teach us how to farm, but this never happened again. They told us to buy fertilizer, but it costs R 7* or more a bag, and us starving people, we have no money. . . .

We aren't the only ones. Everyone around here is the same. It's so bad, there are as many people who don't have land as those who do. Only the people who've already paid all the fees for schools and residence plots get land to farm. And costs are so high—it's R 40 for school, R 21 for water, R 1 for the plot—who can pay?

We grow mealies, watermelons, pumpkins and beans around the house. But it isn't nearly enough to feed us and so we have to buy our food from the shop. We also have three chickens. Sometimes we get eggs. But the chickens are thin, so mostly not.

There are seven of us—me, my husband and my five children. They're at school, but if things stay so bad some will have to leave. My husband works at the ferrochrome mine. I don't know how much he earns. He doesn't give me any cash, he only buys what he thinks is necessary. Often there is no money in the house.

When this happens I borrow from the neighbours. People here are good. They do lend money if they have. We have helped each other. It's all there is. [From *Working Women*, Sached Trust, Ravan Press, 1985, by permission of the publishers]

The "homelands" system

Rose lives in a reservation for Africans called Lebowa, some two hundred miles northeast of Johannesburg. It is one of ten reservations made up of fragments and pieces of what were once small African states or "native reserves," which are now called "homelands" or "national units" by the South African government.

---

* About $8.50-$9 in U.S. dollars in 1981, at the time Rose is speaking about.

Homelands are based on the allegedly indelible "tribal identity" of every African in South Africa. The areas called Transkei and Ciskei are for Xhosa; KwaZulu is for Zulus; Lebowa is for the North Sotho; Bophuthatswana for Tswana, etc. (see the map facing page 1).

A homeland is not necessarily a single geographical unit. Bophuthatswana, for example, consists of six distinct areas, Lebowa of six and KwaZulu of ten. In between are sections reserved for white occupation only. Supposedly, the homelands someday all will become independent countries, although independence was not part of the original apartheid concept. Originally the homelands were simply tribal reservations, which in fact is what they have remained. The fiction that they could become countries was invented to defuse international criticism.

The total area of all South African land allocated for occupation by Africans is only 13 percent. And this is the country's poorest land, with soil eroded and overfarmed or too poor to be cultivated. Generally the homelands are without significant mineral deposits. The best farmlands, the mines, the industries, the ports and cities are in so-called "white" South Africa, which allots 87 percent of the country to 15 percent of the population.

Today, half of all Africans in South Africa, 11.6 million people, live in these encampments. The other half live in other areas on the sufferance of the nation that attempted to take away the common South African nationality of all its Africans.

Africans were not consulted in 1959 when the Promotion of Bantu Self-Government Act was passed, stripping away from them their last rights of citizenship. Until 1959, Africans had been represented indirectly in Parliament (even though their right to vote and to stand for Parliament in the Cape Colony had been taken away). Unsatisfactory as this arrangement was, white advocates often voiced Africans' grievances eloquently from the seven "African seats" in Parliament. The elimination of African political rights now became complete.

Urban Africans were told that they could exercise political rights only in their homelands, although most had been born and always lived where they were and had no interest in, or remaining family connection with, a homeland that might be hundreds of miles away. The Xhosa-speaking majority in Cape Town, for example, lives at least 500 miles from the Xhosa homelands.

Aliens in their own land

The homelands were equally unacceptable to rural Africans. The new laws meant that most were now aliens in parts of the country that had most of the jobs, resources, and educational and cultural opportunities. They could travel in white South Africa, which they understandably saw as their country, only by permission. Their citizenship in a so-called "independent" homeland gave them a valueless political right: to elect governments that can be no more than puppets.

Today, Transkei, Ciskei, Bophuthatswana, Venda and Kwa-Ndebele are allegedly independent countries. But no nation in the world has recognized them, not even Swaziland, Lesotho or Botswana, which are heavily pressured to do so as members of the South African Customs Union. Not a single one of these alleged "nations" can balance its budget or feed its people without enormous subsidies from the South African government. In 1983, for example, the Transkei and the Ciskei received 76.7 percent and 82.6 percent of their budgets from South African grants, taxes, customs duties, aid projects and secondment of officials. While South Africa pumps 9 percent of its budget into these areas to try to make them work, it has never been prepared to spend enough to make them viable economies.

Not only are the homelands economic vassals of South Africa, they are extensions of its security-state system as well. All have signed non-aggression pacts with the central government administration in Pretoria and all form part of its regional defense system. The homelands' police and security forces work hand-in-glove with South African officials to combat and destroy resistance forces that are fighting apartheid, especially those connected to the African National Congress. Detention without trial, torture and repression—features of South Africa's regime—are also practiced in the homelands. By shifting to the so-called "independent countries" the burden of repressing dissent and resistance, South Africa rids itself of part of its ugly public image. By governing the homelands through a privileged black elite class that is beholden to it, Pretoria achieves a public relations gain without losing essential white control and domination.

Reservoirs of the poor and desperate

Uprooting and cordoning off South Africa's black people divided Africans politically, keeping them powerless and under white control. Behind this political maneuver, however, lay an economic purpose. A pool of poor and unemployed people who live near or below starvation level are especially vulnerable to a degree of economic exploitation so high that it amounts to forced labor or slavery.

We have seen in Chapter Two that apartheid did not invent the system of migrant labor and "native reserves." British colonial authorities had used pass laws and influx control in the nineteenth century. Mining houses had started the migrant labor system which separated workers from their families; thus the companies were able to pay lower wages to the African miners. The price of labor was also set low by monopolistic practices. The Africans' system of subsistence farming, commercial farming and trading was under assault long before apartheid arrived in 1948. Institutionalized racism was therefore not solely an invention of Afrikaners or of the apartheid system.

What apartheid did was to rigidify and bureaucratize the system of institutional racism. It tried to protect the jobs of white workers by eliminating black competition as much as possible. To the maximum possible extent, Africans were to be kept in the rural areas. But the government was not prepared to spend the massive sums for industrial development that its own experts said would be necessary to make the reserves economically viable.

In the twenty years from 1960 to 1980, less than 300,000 new jobs were created in the reserves and adjacent border areas, but each year some 200,000 additional Africans came onto the job market. No wonder then that the reserves are chronically overcrowded and incapable of supporting their own population. Apartheid has meant not "separate development" but separate underdevelopment.

By 1980 the homelands population had doubled: 8.9 million people were living in abject poverty, up from 4.1 million in 1960. Given the desperate poverty, the doubled population and the overcrowding of the reserves, the apartheid system extracts an extraordinary benefit—cheap and readily exploited labor for the profit of employers.

Super-exploitative industries

Most of the workers in the new "bantustan" or homelands factories are rural women. These factories are sometimes owned by firms from such countries as Israel and Taiwan, which are close allies of South Africa. Through a collective bantustan development corporation, South Africa offers inducements to foreign firms: low rent, rail and port rebates, etc. These factories are not covered by South African laws setting minimum wages and health and safety conditions, protections that have been gained by long years of trade-union organizing and campaigning. So homeland leaders, who keep their own positions and benefits by helping keep the system as the South African government wants it, often act to disrupt and destroy the growing strength of the labor union movement in South Africa itself. In the Ciskei, for example, hundreds of trade union activitists, such as Thozamile Gqweta of the South African Allied Workers' Union (SAAWU) have been detained; SAAWU, a legal registered organization in South Africa, is banned in the Ciskei. Bophuthatswana has banned all unions.[1]

Recently a womens' research team described the situations of bantustan women:

> Some rural women work in bantustan factories under conditions that are almost as bad as those of the farm workers. . . . There are no legally set minimum wages. . . . There have been cases where women were earning [as little as] R 8 a week. . . . Bantustan factory workers are the least protected of all factory workers.
>
> Figures from 1976 showed that more than half of bantustan factory workers were women. . . . Most men were able to get jobs as migrant workers in factories in the towns. It is desperate unemployed women, who have no choice, who do these bantustan factory jobs.[2]

In a KwaZula textile factory

Gugu Mhlongo is one of the top-paid workers at a textile factory in Isithebe, KwaZulu. She stays in this job because she does not have the legal right to work elsewhere.

> I am a superintendent and I am responsible for the workers. I report all grievances to management, and anything else that goes wrong.
>
> I am qualified in the textile industry. In 1981 I worked in one of the factories here in Isithebe and they trained me. It was a six-month training course. We got paid R 18 a week. . . .
>
> Now I am earning R 38 a week. Another woman and myself earn the same—we are the top-paid workers in the factory.

There are mostly women in this place and they earn very low wages.

I would like to go to a better place to work but I don't have any rights to work anywhere else. Also, I have to look after my mother. . . .

If one asks for the workload to be reduced, that person who asks is dismissed instantly. Six or seven women have been dismissed for this reason. Also the wages are very low—it's a big problem. [From *Working Women,* p. 106]

Racial classification

Because apartheid is a pyramid of privilege based on race, it requires a system to determine who is entitled to be at the top, bottom and middle. So each person must be classified.

The Population Registration Act of 1950 was one of the first major pieces of apartheid legislation. One's racial classification at birth, parentage, residence and work rights were all to be recorded in passbooks, today called identity documents. African, "Indian" and "Coloured" persons may be required to produce proper identification anywhere, even in their own homes. Arrest and imprisonment and possible penalties for those found outside their "areas." Freedom to live, work or travel is severely restricted if one is not "white."

Apartheid classifies people into four main groups: "Whites," Blacks," "Coloureds" and "Indians" (or "Asians").

"White" is used for people accepted as of European descent. They are at the top of the pyramid.

"Black" is the current name the government uses to describe Africans, who constitute 70 percent of the population. (Once, Africans were called *Bantu,* and before that, *Natives.*) Blacks are at the bottom of the pyramid.

The pyramid has two middle groups: people of mixed race and people of Indian ancestry. Many people of mixed race dislike the term "Coloured" and refuse to use it, preferring simply to be called "Black" as a symbol of resistance. Many people of Indian descent similarly object to the racist terminology: "I am not an Indian. I am not a citizen of India. I don't belong to that country. I am a South African. PERIOD. And I want my rights." So said an exiled member of the African National Congress.

In recent years, the government has attempted to woo these middle groups by allowing them some apparent privileges. Under the new constitution of 1983 they have the right to vote for their own parliaments, for example, although these bodies are essentially powerless to decide any vital issues. General legislation and actual power rest in white hands.

One member of the "Coloured" branch of Parliament, Allen Hendrikse, formerly a Congregational minister, became the only non-white person in State President Botha's cabinet. Hendrikse was recently shown what his position amounted to. When he tried to swim with friends at a "white" beach, he was ordered by Botha to apologize or resign. He apologized.*

The classification system produces bizarre as well as humiliating results. A person is "white" if he or she "obviously" looks white and is "not generally accepted as Coloured" or is "not in appearance obviously not a white person." Fingernails are peered at; hair subjected to lab tests. In 1984, 795 South Africans were re-classified, generally in attempts to move up in the pyramid. Thus, 518 former Coloureds became Whites, and 89 Africans became Coloureds in that year.

Relocation, or order in the crazy house

Although apartheid pays economic benefits to the minority, it does not rely on market forces to make segregation work. Apartheid imposes order by bureaucratic controls, by political manipulation and, if need be, by sheer force. Nowhere is apartheid's essential brutality revealed more clearly than in the policy of making room for white occupation by removing Africans from areas where they have lived for generations and dumping them in barren reservations.

U.S. reporter Joseph Lelyveld describes the forced removal of one family to the "homeland" of Kwa Ndebele:

> At a place called Kwaggafontein, I came upon the Nduli family, who had just been evicted from their kraal [home] on a white farm . . . about fifty miles away. I found them with their paltry belongings on a plot white officials had staked out on a grassy hillside, which was fast being blighted by squalid shanties. Rose Nduli was literally sitting on the veld [field] while her son, Kleinbooi, wearing a brown shoe on his right foot and on his left a black boot laced with copper wire,

---

* Hendrikse subsequently resigned from the Cabinet in 1987 because of his humiliation.

chipped away with a shovel at the dry stuccolike earth in order to prepare the ground for a shelter. Kleinbooi said they knew none of their neighbors. He knew that he had landed at a place called Kwaggafontein, but he hadn't been told that KwaNdebele was supposed to have deep significance for him as his homeland. When I asked him who brought him there, he replied simply, "GG." The initials are the first two letters of the official license plates on the government trucks used to move blacks out of white areas. Throughout the rural Transvaal and Natal, it has become the universal shorthand among blacks for the white government, its pervasive authority, and its arbitrary ways, which seem to be beyond ordinary comprehension. GG is as unpredictable as natural calamity. GG scoops you up when you least expect it and drops you somewhere you have never seen, leaving it to you to patch together the torn and ragged pattern of a life. And like natural calamity, it evokes depression and resignation, rather than resentment. "The law is the law," Rose Nduli said, "and we have nothing to say about it." [From *Move Your Shadow*, p. 123]

The crazy rationale for KwaNdebele itself makes no sense either politically or economically. It was pieced together in 1980 from white farms in order to create an independent homeland for Ndebele people. But very few Ndebele people are left in South Africa; most are in Zimbabwe. So the homeland is simply a vast resettlement camp for some 200,000 blacks arbitrarily sent there from Transvaal cities and towns.

In order to make KwaNdebele an effective reserve for urban workers, the government had to provide transport for their fifty- to eighty-mile commute to Pretoria. Some commuters must get up at two in the morning in order to be at work by seven. Eventually the government had to subsidize the bus company with $1,000 a year per commuter. The money could have been better spent on inner-city housing, but that would violate the apartheid plan. Journalist Lelyveld commented:

The KwaNdebele bus subsidy—the government's largest single expense in the development of this homeland—was higher than the KwaNdebele gross domestic product. This is basic apartheid economics. It had to be so high because KwaNdebele, a state supposedly on the way to independence, was utterly devoid of a productive economy or resources.

The racial doctrine sets the priorities: First you invent the country; then, if you can, an economy.[3]

Nobody knows exactly how many people like the Nduli family have been arbitrarily moved out of their homes and dumped on some barren patch of ground, but the total runs into the millions. In 1983, the Surplus People Project estimated that 3.5 million such removals had taken place since 1960.[4]

No more sharecroppers

Over a million of these removals affected tenants or laborers on white farms. Some had to leave when the labor-tenant system ended. After the Land Act of 1913, Africans could no longer rent land from white owners for cash. They therefore became labor tenants, meaning that they would work for a white farmer for a period, usually three or four months, in return for working a portion of the land for themselves. By the 1940s, however, white farmers, who wanted no African competition, lobbied for the abolition of labor tenancy. Under apartheid this abolition has largely been accomplished. Formerly semi-independent African farmers have been forced to become farm workers, paid bottom-of-the-barrel wages.[5]

Black laborers on white farms have no secure tenure. Often they are made "redundant" when the employer decides to reduce the labor force by substituting a capital-intensive crop, such as irrigated wheat, which is worked mainly by machinery. Others leave because they simply cannot live on such low wages. A woman named Alice describes her own experience of farm work, remembering the days of labor tenancy:

> The wages here are R 20 a month [in 1982]. We survive because we are helped by our children in the location [an African township near a city or town]. Without them, I don't know. There is a farm on that side where the white man pays the people R 10 a month. No, what can they eat? How can you live? And children too. That white man is playing with people—R 10 a month. For men!
>
> The whites have money. Really and truly they have lots. They have cars and lorries and airplanes. And what can we buy? Nothing. . . .
>
> We have always suffered on the farms, but things were better before. Before, we could plough. Our parents worked

on the six-month system [labor tenancy with six months of unpaid labor]. But they ploughed and they got mealies [ears of corn, a dietary staple]. Now things have changed. They don't want you to plough, and yet the money is too little. . . .

If people have no children in Jo'burg what will they eat? It's because of this that some of the children are swollen up. Yes, they swell up and die from hunger. . . .

If all our children go for better work in Jo'burg, they will fire us from here. We will have to go to the reserves. That place is terrible. It's all hills. . . . It's full and full of stones. People go there. What else can they do? they say that they are starving. Oh Jesus, there is famine there. . . .

Those boers who used us for free [under labor tenancy]— what will they do for us now that we are old? Nothing, niks. [From *Working Women*, p. 105]

Black Spots

"Black spots" are African communities outside the homelands in areas which the government decides must be for white occupation only.* Most are properties that Africans held in freehold for generations before the Land Act of 1913 carved up the country. Some pieces are held in trust by church missionary societies, some by single African farmers who lease them out, and some are owned communally. In the 1960s, 350 such pockets amounted to half a million acres. Gradually, these communities are being smashed. Government statements portray these removals as voluntary or else as carried out with compassion and respect. Such propaganda hides the ugly truth.

Francis Wilson, a well-known economist, describes what happened at Mogopa (pronounced Mahopa) in western Transvaal:

The village had been bulldozed by the government as a prelude to moving the people from land they had been able to buy before the Land Act of 1913 . . . It was lovely land, well watered, and stocked with cattle. The people were to be moved to a place called Pachsdraai in the independent "homeland" of Bophuthatswana. I saw the stone houses that the people had painstakingly built up over the years. I met the village elders gathered anxiously to discuss how best to prevent the great evil that was looming over them—the

---

* About half of all blacks in South Africa live outside the homelands.

destruction of their homes and their community. I heard about the water pumps that had been removed and about the buses that were no longer coming. Aninka Claasens of the anti-apartheid organization, Black Sash, explains what happened next: "What does the state do once [it has] smashed the schools, stopped the transport, cut off the water, threatened force—and the people refuse to move . . . It waits. . . .

Still the people refused to move. After the first demolitions they regrouped and set about the reconstruction of Mogopa. They rebuilt the school from rubble. Then, in the early hours of 14 February 1984, Mogopa was surrounded by armed government police. At 4:00 a.m., the people were informed through loud hailers that they must load their possessions into trucks and go to Pachsdraai. The residents were not allowed to leave their houses. The government-appointed chief, Jacob More, took the police and the officials to the houses of the leaders first, who were handcuffed and put into police vans. Their families refused to pack. . . . Women were carried into the lorries and buses. Children were loaded with the furniture. . . . All of this happened in the presence of scores of armed policemen with dogs. . . . People caught standing together outside their houses were beaten with batons. . . . No outsiders were allowed into Mogopa, excepting the police, of course, and the white farmers who had free access in and out to buy the people's livestock at a tenth of its value. [From *South Africa: The Cordoned Heart*, p. 16, used by permission of the publisher, W.W. Norton]

Urban relocations

For years, South Africa has tried to keep Africans away from the cities. As far back as 1922, a government commission argued that urban areas were "white man's creation." Blacks were to enter only to "minister to the needs of the white man." As mining and manufacturing grew, however, the whites' need for labor grew. More and more Africans wanted to leave the poor rural areas and settle with their families in the cities, where the jobs were. But this desire contradicted government policy.

The pass law system under which 17 million Africans have been prosecuted in the last seventy years has been one device to remove "surplus" Africans from cities. Another has been government's refusal to build housing for Africans in the cities or even in "commuter homelands" like KwaNdebele.

The result is enormous overcrowding in urban African townships. In Soweto, the black suburb of Johannesburg, twenty to thirty people often live in a four-room house. People sometimes build shacks on their own, which then are torn down when discovered by the authorities.[6]

A glaring example of this conflict between apartheid policy and the human needs of Africans is Cape Town's Crossroads settlement. Cape Town is a "Coloured Preference Area"; that is, Africans may work in Cape Town only if no "Coloured" person is available. But in today's economy, 200,000 African families live as "squatters" in Cape Town, because they need work that the "homelands" can't provide and because they do not want to live in the single-sex hostels designated for African workers. Government policy is to provide no housing for families; wives and children belong in the homelands—they are not permitted to live with their husbands and fathers.

In order to stay together, African workers and their families built Crossroads as a self-help remedy. Although the houses were shacks, the people themselves built them. Crime was low, employment was high and children were nutritionally three times as healthy as their country relatives in the homelands.

The government has been trying to get rid of Crossroads and other squatter communities since 1977. The people, however, organized resistance. When the government bulldozed their shacks, the squatters rebuilt them. In 1985, after a series of confrontations and a battle in which twenty-two people died defending their community, Gerrit Viljoen, the government's minister of Cooperation and Development, promised to "upgrade" Crossroads. It was then announced that Africans could live and work in Cape Town for eighteen months if they moved to Khayelitsha, a new location to be built on barren sands some thirty miles out of town. Few were willing to accept such an "upgrading".[7]

As in other places, the government used a black minority as collaborators to justify and execute removals in Crossroads. They were called the "witdoeke" (white bands) because they wore white strips of cloth on their heads and arms.

First, the government held elections for a local community council, which 90 percent of the community boycotted because they already knew who their leaders were. The police then detained, interrogated and tortured the real leadership, broke into houses and even fired on people gathered for worship.

The witdoeke evicted those of their political opponents that had not been jailed, forcing them to find shelter in outlying areas of Crossroads. Finally, on a Sunday in May 1985, the combined witdoeke and government forces attacked.

A group of church observers witnessed what happened. In a statement published by the Western Province Christian Council, they described some of the scenes. The South African Security Forces made extensive use of tear gas, but the witdoeke groups were never teargassed. Nor did the security forces try to disperse the heavily armed witdoeke groups, although residents who tried to retrieve belongings from their homes were constantly dispersed. Witdoeke gangs burned down shacks, looted possessions, and actually assaulted other Crossroads residents while the security forces stood by and watched.[8]

A radically unequal society

When criticized for apartheid, a typical government response is to compare the lot of black people in South Africa to those living elsewhere in Africa. Such comments try to deflect attention away from the fact that, unlike the rest of Africa, South Africa is a relatively industrialized and developed country. Hunger and poverty are indeed common throughout Africa. But amid these and other problems of the continent, South Africa is unique because massive and terrible poverty exists in it side-by-side with massive and incredible profits and wealth. And these two extremes are symbiotic: that is, the extreme of poverty helps to produce the extreme of wealth.

In 1970, the 20 percent of South Africa's population who were the richest owned 75 percent of the wealth. The poorest 40 percent of South Africans get only 8 percent of the total income.[9] Although blacks now make up two-thirds of the labor force, they receive only one-third of the total wages. Whites, who are now only a fifth of the labor force, receive three-fifths of total wages.

These disparities are not the result of impersonal market forces— but of deliberate planning. That, too, makes South Africa unique. Institutionalized racism exists elsewhere (including the United States and Canada), but in South Africa it is the law of the land. To be poor and black in South Africa is to be treated by law with utter disrespect.

Death at an early age

Apartheid often means death at an early age. In the homelands, there is one doctor for every 14,000 people in the Transkei, one for every 17,000 in Bophuthatswana, and one for every 19,000 in Gazankulu. These are figures comparable to those in the poorest, least-developed countries in the world. South African whites, on the other hand, are served by doctors at a one to 330 ratio.

Given these facts, it is hardly surprising that, overall, whites can expect to live an average 72.3 years while life expectancy for Africans is only 58.9 years. In rural areas, black life expectancy is dramatically worse.

One black child out of ten dies before he or she is a year old; for white children the figure is one out of fifty—a dramatic difference. In the homelands and the resettlement camps, the infant mortality rate is 20-25 percent. Over half of the black children who die before they are five are killed by malnutrition.[10]

Unequal Education

When "Bantu" education was introduced in the 1950s, Hendrik Verwoerd, then Minister of Native Affairs, outlined its purpose:

> When I have control of Native Education I will reform it so that the Natives will be taught from childhood to realize that equality with Europeans is not for them. . . . People who believe in equality are not desirable teachers for Natives.
>
> The school must equip [the African] to meet the demands which the economic life will impose on him [sic]. . . . There is no place for him above the level of certain forms of labor. . . . For that reason it is of no avail for him to receive a training which has as its aim absorption in the European community.[11]

While the government now argues that its policy has changed, the change is primarily rhetorical. The educational system remains segregated and unequal. Schools are designated for particular racial groups. The only exceptions are private schools, including church schools, which now admit some black Africans, "Indians" and "Coloureds" to what were once purely white institutions.

The amount spent to educate a white child in 1982-83 was 1,385 Rands (roughly U.S. $1,662.) To educate a black child, the government spent only 8 percent of that, R 113.19 (U.S. $135). While the government says it wants to provide equal education, there is no evidence that it is prepared to spend the sums required. Among whites, military expenditures for defending apartheid are more popular than the prospect of increasing expenditures for equal education—an estimated boost from the current 18 percent of the budget to at least 30 percent. Although a government-appointed commission recommended a single education system with uniform standards, the government continues to reject it.

The percentage of African and "Coloured" schoolchildren in the last grade of high school is only one quarter of the percentage of white schoolchildren enrolled in that grade. One reason so many African children drop out of school is that their teachers are far less qualified. In 1985 only 15 percent had a matriculation certificate. Another reason for dropouts is that parents cannot afford to pay school fees and purchase the required books and uniforms. Half of all African and "Coloured" children leave school after only four years of education; most of these are unable to read and write. Almost six million South African adults are illiterate—almost none of them white. It is easy to understand why only 12.25 percent of Africans who take university entrance exams pass them, while almost 50 percent of whites go on to higher education.[12]

African teachers and students have devised ways to combat even such a willfully skewed and unequal educational system from within. Mbulelo Mzamane, who took part in the students' revolt of 1976, recalls a particular teacher, Pakade, who helped create Black Consciousness in the classroom:

> At school the majority of us deeply resented being taught Afrikaans. We preferred to communicate in our street dialect, called tsotsi-taal, the lingua franca of black youth. . . .
>
> In class, Pakade's fertile imagination transformed every-thing it dwelt upon, including the drabbest material of the Afrikaans language and culture. . . . He possessed an essentially satirical mind and his peculiar blend of humour brought even the most absurd situations featuring blacks, with which literature in that language abounds, into very sharp relief. We saw the Afrikaaner . . . as paranoid and egocentric in the extreme. Here were people recreating the black world in their own image, without bothering to find out whether this corresponded to the objective reality.
>
> For comparison Pakade made us read other writers on Africa. We noticed the same tendency among white writers of English expression, although here we found the same

prejudices couched in more guarded terms. But the tone of condescension, of paternalism, was unmistakable. . . .

[W]e knew very well that for examination purposes we needed to modify our views drastically. . . . Our ability to supply dumb answers, to turn into obsequious samboes, to transform our whole personalities instantaneously when conditions so dictated—these qualities had been nurtured in us very early in our youth. . . . [An excerpt from Mbulelo Vizihungo Mzamane's *Children of Soweto*, p. 7; used by permission]

Unequal Employment

The economic situation of some of South Africa's oppressed people has improved modestly in the last fifteen years. Beginning in 1973 with a rash of illegal strikes in Durban, labor militancy has grown steadily. The government has been forced to recognize that black people could not all be sent back to homelands but were in fact a growing part of the industrial and mining workforce. Whites were unable to fill all the skilled slots reserved for them. Owners of businesses found ways to employ blacks, "Coloureds" and "Indians" even when it was not legal to do so—workers from these groups were far more numerous, not as well organized into unions and often were desperate for any job they could get. "Job Reservation," the legal system of keeping certain jobs for whites only, ended in June 1983.

Most of the better-paid jobs are still in white hands although the overall wage gap between whites and other races has narrowed. Still, government statistics for 1984 show the average white wage-earner earning 1,300 Rands per month while the average black wage-earner was making 330 Rands, less than a quarter of white earnings. The biggest gap is in the mining industry, where African earnings are only 19 percent of white earnings. White miners have refused to allow the opening of all jobs to all races.

No one knows for sure how many people are unemployed in South Africa today, but estimates run as high as 3 million black Africans out of work. In the homelands, between one-quarter and one-half of the people who want to work simply can't. Almost 1.5 million homeland people have no income at all, and 9 million live in absolute poverty.[13]

Women bear a double burden

In traditional African societies, the man did the work requiring greater physical strength, including hunting, heavy construction, herding and fighting. He was also the decision maker. The council of elders, the adults charged with advising the chief, was an all-male group. Women were under the guardianship of their fathers and then their husbands.

Women's work was hard. They were in charge of growing the food, including weeding, hoeing and even plowing. They drew the water and chopped the firewood, cooked the food and took care of the children. They made the household pots and utensils and added decorative designs to the houses.[14]

With the discovery of diamonds and gold, people who had lived as self-sufficient farmers were forced into new patterns. Because the central government laid taxes on their "huts," which had to be paid in cash, recruiters from the mining houses found African men willing to become migrant laborers. Men moved to cities and towns to earn cash wages. They seldom saw their families, often resorting to prostitutes and alcohol to make life bearable. When they returned to their villages, they often felt "citified," no longer able to participate in traditional life.

With African population growing while their land use was restricted, farming could no longer produce enough food or money to sustain a family. Yet women and children were supposed to stay in the rural areas and live off the land. "Influx Control" laws stated that women who were "unqualified" (qualifications had no relation to competence) had no right to seek work in towns and cities. But women moved to town in spite of the laws.

At first, women were not allowed to work in factories. Even domestic and laundry jobs were for men. Women earned money selling, brewing beer and by prostitution. Then they began to be employed in domestic service and in clothing and food preparation industries. Today, although employed in a wide variety of jobs, African women are the worst-paid and least protected of all of South Africa's workers. As we have seen, homelands factories offer low pay, long hours, heavy work and very little security.

For African women who work in urban areas, the burden is double. Often husbands do not understand or appreciate what working a "double shift" means. They may expect their wives to follow the traditional pattern—to do all the household chores, to be obedient and continue not to participate in decisions—even though the circumstances have changed drastically. The women may, in fact, be doing important political and labor union work in addition to working at the office or factory and at home.

An example of a "double-shift" woman is Louise Yekwa, a school teacher in Alexandra, a township near Johannesburg. As a teacher, her working hours are short. But Louise is also studying for a matriculation certificate which will enable her to get university level qualifications.

> Now I'm teaching in Alex. I'm teaching higher primary—general science and health education, Afrikaans and needlework. Ooh, it's demanding. But I like teaching. As compared with other jobs there are some advantages. Because you knock off at about ten past two. Then if you've got some work to do you remain until three o'clock, then you can go home, look after the kids. . . .
>
> At home I don't have anyone to help me. I have to do everything because my kids are still young. When I'm not at home my husband helps. When I'm at home—nothing. . . . He only cooks when I am out—maybe if I'm away on a school tour. But he will never cook when I am around. . . .
>
> I'm studying for matric because I want to get promoted. I don't want to become a principal. I just want to be an inspectress. I study after supper. I forget about TV and radio. Then I sit on my books. Sometimes I sleep early. I go to sleep at eight o'clock and wake up at about twelve and study till morning. . . . [Excerpt from *Working Women*, p. 121]

Summing it up

We have seen how apartheid has deliberately divided the country, giving power and privileges to a minority at the expense of the majority. From its roots in a doctrine of white supremacy, this racist ideology has grown into a rigid, legal, bureaucratically planned system.

Apartheid is a sin, because sin means, in part, the hostile separation of people from one another. Apartheid is an idol, because it creates a national system which claims that racial domination is God's will. The wages of this sin is death—literally for those who are dominated and spiritually for the dominators, because of their unbelief in the humanity of others.

Chapter Five:
Does the Piper Call the Tune?

[Divestment seems] a wonderful moral cause and everybody feels good about it. But it's not going to bring down the rapid demise of the Government. The Government will plod on with its incremental changes, or, if things get really tough . . . close down the hatches, become self-sufficient and go into a situation approximating martial law." [Helen Suzman, white liberal member of the South African Parliament, as quoted in *The New York Times*, June 3, 1986]

Helen Suzman has for years opposed sanctions* against South Africa, so it is not surprising that she should attack them as counterproductive even though her own methods of transforming apartheid through white-led reforms have not worked either. She did, however, correctly predict what the South African Government would do. Since the enactment of partial trade sanctions by the United States Congress in October 1986, South Africa has continued to be defiant and intransigent.

Based on this limited experience, some critics like Helen Suzman now argue that sanctions have proved a failure. But others maintain that it is too soon to judge, and that even partial sanctions can work, especially if they are globally imposed, broadened and effectively enforced. Central to the discussion of these questions is the issue of South Africa's self-sufficiency: can it "go it alone" or is it so dependent on the outside world that international sanctions can be used as one lever for needed change?

This chapter will examine in some detail the South African

---

* We use *sanctions* to refer to economic actions mandated by national or international laws or regulations to deprive South Africa of some economic value in order to persuade it to comply with norms or demands that the sanctioning nation(s) sets. *Divestment* is the selling of securities in a corporation or other entity doing business in South Africa as a protest against its doing so. *Disinvestment* is the action of the business entity itself in shutting down its operations in or with South Africa: withdrawing capital or technology; selling or closing plants or offices; and ending sales, financing, use of trademarks, logos, patents or other property.

economy, showing that it is much more dependent on foreign capital, trade and technology than Ms. Suzman and others recognize. South Africa's economy is very strong but by no means self-sufficient. We will also look at the extent of United States and Canadian investment in and trade with South Africa to see what involvement these countries have in supporting apartheid.

An advanced but backward country

Western media often portray apartheid solely as an aberration stemming from the Christian Nationalism of Afrikaners. But English-speaking whites have also been supporters of apartheid's institutionalized racism, as we shall see when we look at the role foreign and domestic capital plays in South Africa. Apartheid is like a three-legged stool: one leg is Afrikaner racist ideology, the other two are the foreign and domestic capital whose investments support it and profit from it.

We have seen that the system of migrant labor and the expropriation of African farm land pre-date apartheid and were instituted by capitalist interests. At first, foreign bankers and investors alone financed the mining boom. Today South Africa has generated its own domestic capital and can finance many of its own developments, but it is not by any means self-sufficient. Having become in many ways an "advanced" country, South Africa still also resembles many "third-world" countries in its dependence on exports of minerals and on imports of money and technological capital. Here, as in other third-world countries, a prosperous elite enjoys the benefits of development while a large majority of the population suffers because it is deprived of them.

One measure of a country's development status is domestic manufacturing. By 1984 South Africa's output from manufacturing had reached 22 percent of its Gross Domestic Product*, a percentage not very different from that of Great Britain or the United States. But other features make South Africa's a "backward" economy. It produces little heavy machinery, aircraft or such sophisticated technical equipment as computers—all needed to compete as a modern developed economy. In fact, South Africa's reliance on outside suppliers for these products has been increasing.

Half of what South Africa imported in 1910 was consumer goods such as food, clothing, and textiles.[1] By 1975, South Africa had

---

* Gross Domestic Product is the net output of internal production at market prices. Income from external investment must be added to obtain Gross National Product.

become relatively self-sufficient in manufacturing these goods. Instead, 53 percent of South Africa's imports were machinery and transport equipment, compared to 20 percent at the end of World War II. By 1983 the figure was closer to two-thirds of the import total.[2] The vast majority of capital goods and equipment used in South Africa today are in fact imported. Although South Africa has become a manufacturing country, the goods it makes are largely for domestic consumption or for sale in nearby countries.

Another critical import is oil. South Africa has been unable to find natural petroleum on its own territory. Its offshore explorations so far have found natural gas but not oil.

Gold still buys a lot

On the export side of the ledger, exports of raw and semi-finished materials are extremely important. Three-quarters of South Africa's exports consist of minerals and agricultural products like grain, sugar, fruit, wine and vegetables.

Gold is critically important because it is the source of major foreign exchange. In 1983 gold paid for almost half of South Africa's imports. While South Africa often makes a strong case for its crucial role in supplying the West with such strategic minerals as chrome and platinum, sales of these and other non-gold minerals were only a quarter of total mineral exports; the rest was gold.

South Africa cannot buy the locomotives, computers, airplanes, mining and industrial machines it requires without the foreign exchange it gets from selling minerals. Trade, therefore, is vital to South Africa's ability to grow and prosper as a powerful state. Conversely, a cut-off of trade would deprive South Africa of some of its technological power—power that is used internally to dominate and repress its own population.

By 1984, the United States had replaced Great Britain as South Africa's most important trading partner, with a total trade approaching $5 billion. By 1986, however, U.S. exports to South Africa had fallen from $2.27 billion to $1.16 billion. Automatic data processing equipment, aircraft, office machinery, parts for road vehicles and tractors, and organic chemicals continued to be the leading U.S. exports to South Africa. But what the U.S. imported—primarily silver, platinum group metals, precious stones, uranium and ferroalloys—were $2.8 billion, close to the 1984 levels.[3]

By comparison with the U.S., Canada's trade with South Africa is not very significant. Canadian exports to South Africa were 153 million in Canadian dollars in 1985, a falloff of 25 percent from the previous year. The most significant, sulphur, amounted to almost half of all exports. The most important technological exports were drilling, excavating and mining machinery worth $7.9 million (Canadian). South African imports into Canada were $227 million (Canadian); the most important items were metal ores, concentrates and scrap, raw sugar, and fresh fruits and berries.[4]

U.S. law now forbids importing products that South African government parastatal* corporations produce: iron, steel, uranium, coal, textiles, arms, ammunition and military vehicles, as well as sugar and farm products. But President Reagan has exempted ten strategic minerals from these sanctions, including chromium, ferrochromium, cobalt, natural industrial diamonds, manganese, and platinum group metals. While South Africa claims to be the world's leading supplier of such strategic minerals, its real advantage lies in its lower prices, which reflect its cheap labor policies. The U.S. government has shown little interest in shifting to alternative suppliers. The issue is price, not availability. Eight of the ten materials could be obtained from other countries in southern Africa if a commitment were made to develop the resources of independent, black-ruled nations.[5]

When the balance tips

Although South Africa's sales of gold and other minerals normally provide adequate foreign exchange, there have been, and continue to be, occasions when South Africa cannot manage its balance of payments in this way. At these crucial moments, Pretoria turns to the international banking world for help: it depends on foreign capital to shore up its economy.

For example, in the mid-'70s a combination of factors led to such a crisis. In 1974 South Africa experienced a recession, in part because a world-wide economic slump reduced its earnings. In addition, the price it had to pay for oil jumped dramatically. After Arab and African states imposed an oil embargo, South Africa was forced to buy on the expensive "spot" market from unscrupulous dealers and from Arab countries willing to deal under the table.

South Africa was also faced with rising military costs. In October 1975, it had launched an invasion of Angola in order to overturn a socialist government which had come to power after the fall

---

* Parastatals are government-owned business corporations that have their own semi-autonomous managements.

of the Portugese colonial system. In Rhodesia, it was maintaining another army to fight against African nationalism. At home, it was faced with popular discontent and a rash of strikes.

In response to this crisis, South Africa borrowed money extensively, especially on the Euro-dollar market. U.S. banks tripled their loans to South Africa in the 1974-76 period.

Then, fortuitously, the world price of gold rose to over $800 an ounce as individuals and countries wrestling with inflation bought gold as a hedge in 1979-80. Revenues from international loans and from gold sales enabled the South African government to undertake such massive strategic projects as building two huge facilities that make oil from coal and increasing its production of arms, necessary because of U.N. sanctions against arms sales to South Africa.

Very little of the money that came into South Africa either from loans or increased gold prices went toward improving the standard of living for African workers. Wage increases for Africans have been gained by increased strength in the trade union movement— not because of foreign loans, investments or sales of minerals.

Power to dominate the region

Because of international pressure from churches, human rights groups and others as well as some purely financial conderations, many foreign investors are now "disinvesting" by selling out their South African operations to South African companies. To know what effect this disinvestment is having, we need to understand South Africa's domestic capital structure. Foreign investors often sell out to South Africans who have the capital to buy rather than simply ceasing all business in South Africa. In these cases, disinvesting companies may be strengthening a monopolistic economy and thus strengthening South Africa's grip on its black neighbors. Furthermore, because of its internal and international linkages, South Africa's capital is not readily isolated. If we understand this situation, we will see why it is important that comprehensive *sanctions* encompassing trade, technology, licensing and all forms of investment are much more important than the limited and ineffectual *disinvestment* that has taken place so far.

While the mining and manufacturing revolution in South Africa was initially financed by foreign capital, South Africa today draws strength from its own capital, making it more independent than it was in the early days. Since the Sharpeville massacre in 1960,

South African business has become increasingly monopolistic. Companies have consolidated their power by buyouts and mergers, have centralized their managements, and have interlocked their businesses through common ownership and directors.

Banks and finance houses have moved into mining and manufacturing. Manufacturers have gone into banking, finance, trade and mining. Afrikaner companies, once regarded as newcomers, have bought into non-Afrikaner companies and vice versa. Multinational corporations have bought into local companies; in some cases they have sold out to local companies but have retained a stake through licensing arrangements and buy-back options. Trading in stocks of South African companies, particularly those which produce gold and diamonds, has increased dramatically on world stock exchanges, especially in response to inflation in the 1970s.

Today, eight big conglomerates own 61.7 percent of all corporate assets in South Africa that are not owned by the state. The largest of these are Anglo-American and SANLAM, who owned 23.6 percent and 16.8 percent by 1981. Recent acquisitions by Anglo-American from such foreign multinationals as Ford and Barclays Bank have probably made these percentages even higher. Every "big eight" conglomerate has shares or directorships in one or more of the others. Parastatal corporations own a quarter of the assets held by the top 138 companies.[5]

The Anglo-American giant

The top five South African mining houses all belong to the Anglo-American conglomerate group. This South African entity either controls or has a substantial minority share in five of the top ten manufacturing companies. It has interests in seven of the top twenty banks, including Standard and Barclays.

Anglo-American is also an important actor in the economy of neighboring black states. It controls Zimbabwe's production of sugar, beer and coal, dominates its fertilizer industry and has a big stake in processing of maize (corn) and other grains and food crops. Through De Beers diamond mines, Anglo-American is the major player in Botswana's diamond industry and in a copper-nickel mine that is the biggest employer in that country. This inordinate economic influence is related to South Africa's intentions toward neighboring countries, as we shall see in Chapter Seven.

The influence of Anglo-American, which is one of the top international corporations, is truly enormous. Through De Beers, Anglo controls the world's major diamond mining and marketing operations except for those in the Soviet Union. It is involved in 250 different companies active in at least 22 countries. In addition to the operations in Botswana and Zimbabwe mentioned above, Anglo-American is also active in the southern African countries of Namibia, Angola, Tanzania, Lesotho, Swaziland and Zambia. Nor are all Anglo-American operations confined to Africa.

Many U.S. citizens would probably be surprised to learn Anglo-American is the biggest foreign investor in the United States.* It has substantial stakes in Phibro, a commodity trader which in turn owns the biggest private investment bank in the U.S., Salomon Brothers. It owns a majority interest in the Englehard Group, which includes in its operations refining, fabricating and trading precious metals, especially gold and platinum. It has major connections with Newmont Mining, a U.S.-based international mining company that supplied some of the original capital to start Anglo-American. Through MINORCO, a subsidiary in the tax haven of Bermuda, Anglo-American draws U.S. investment income of $26.57 billion.

In Canada, through AMCAN, Anglo-American owns a controlling interest in Hudson Bay Mining and Smelting, a major Canadian mining conglomerate. Whitehorse Copper Mines is also Anglo-controlled. An Anglo-American subsidiary specializing in diamond and tungsten-tipped drilling tools supplies drill bits to Canadian mining companies through Boart Canada. International Nickel of Canada has major links and contracts with Anglo-American.[6]

Its connections with international mining companies as well as banking and industrial concerns make Anglo-American an important link in a chain of international organizations that control a huge proportion of the productive resources of the world.[7]

The role of foreign capital

While domestic capital has grown and multiplied, South Africa still relies on foreign investment to carry it past crises. This reliance can seem deceptively small. In 1984, it has been estimated, South

---

* The Anglo-American Corporation was formed in 1917 to tap the expanding capital markets of the United States, hence its name. J. P. Morgan and Co. became an important shareholder and Guaranty Trust its banker. Previously, the controlling organizers of Anglo, the Oppenheimer family, had drawn on British and German money for financing. Anglo-American has therefore always been an international company with a headquarters in South Africa.

Africa had total foreign liabilities of 42 billion Rands, amounting to 40 percent of its Gross Domestic Product; other estimates place the figure somewhat lower. But to understand the significance of foreign investment we need to know not simply how much of it there is but also the role it plays in making South Africa strong.

First, how much do these foreign investments amount to? Foreign investments are made in South Africa in three ways: direct investment, portfolio investment and loans.

Direct investment is an investment in a South African enterprise that is effectively controlled by a foreign corporation, partnership, or individual. Definition of control varies. The United States defines control as ownership of at least 10 percent of the enterprise. U.S. direct investment figures do not report investments in South Africa through a foreign subsidiary of a U.S. company. For Canada, direct ownership means control of 51 percent of a company, but Canada also lists control via third parties as well as effective, but not direct, control. Furthermore, the statistics don't reflect certain technical evasions. IBM, for example, dominates the South African computer market but it is no longer a direct investor; it has entered into an agency and joint venture agreement with a local company formed to carry on its business. This pattern will be used increasingly by U.S. companies to evade public pressure for real disinvestment, i.e., a cessation of all business with South Africa.[8]

The largest source of foreign direct investment is Great Britain. Almost half of the foreign-controlled firms and almost half of the direct foreign investment in South Africa are British. This dominance is primarily the legacy of British imperialism.

Portfolio investment consists of shares of stock or other securities in South African enterprises held by foreign persons. These investments provide dividends, interest or other income but not a controlling interest. The precise total of such investment varies with the prices of such shares on the stock exchanges of the world and is difficult to estimate.

Loans are amounts borrowed by South African governmental entities, by private businesses and by banks. As of December 1986, the Bank for International Settlements reported that banks reporting to it had loans to South Africa of over $16 billion (U.S.). There are, in addition, loans such as trade credits and other non-bank transactions. Authoritative journals of finance place the total of South Africa's foreign debt at $23 to $24 billion.[9]

In March 1987, South Africa signed an agreement rescheduling payments of its foreign debts over a three-year period. Although creditor banks had been expected to press Pretoria for stepped-up repayments, repayments will apparently be no more than $1.4 billion in the next three years. Nor did the international bankers exact any political concessions for their leniency, notwithstanding the pleas of international church leaders.[10]

North American investment in South Africa

United States-based companies are the second largest investors in South Africa, with some 20 percent of the total foreign investment. At the end of 1986, U.S. direct investment stood at $1.4 billion, representing some 240 U.S. firms.

In comparison, in 1982, when the present crisis in South Africa could be said to have begun, U.S. direct investment was $2.28 billion. But the recent decrease was caused almost entirely by a decline in the value of the Rand, not by disinvestment. As the Rand's worth slid from over one U.S. dollar to less than forty cents, companies revalued the profits they had put back into their South African companies and came up with substantial paper losses[11]

One estimate is that the real disinvestment in the 1982-85 period was not more than $50 million. For 1986, U.S. Commerce Department data shows a decline of only $11 million, most of it from paper capital gains and losses due to exchange rate fluctuations.[12]

U.S. investments pass through Canada

Turning to Canadian figures, we find that Canadian-controlled investment in South Africa amounted to $962 million (Canadian) in 1982. This total included subsidiaries with at least 51 percent ownership (direct), partially owned but controlled subsidiaries and indirectly owned South African enterprises through a third party.

Of the Canadian direct investments in South Africa, which amounted to $200 million, only $44 million was actually held by Canadian enterprises controlled by Canadian investors. The other $156 million was controlled by investors outside Canada. Ford Motor Company, for example, has made all its investments in South Africa through the Ford Motor Company of Canada in order to take advantage of certain tax treaties. That investment does not show up in U.S. statistics as an investment in South Africa; it is listed as an investment in Canada. It does show up in the

Canadian figures as a Canadian direct investment in South Africa. A preliminary estimate for 1984 showed Canadian direct investment was $135 million, a decrease of $65 million from 1982. How much of this represents actual disinvestment is not clear.[13]

The most important area of "portfolio" investments are the shares or depository receipts in South African gold and diamond companies purchased by U.S. and Canadian investors. One estimate placed South African mining shares owned by U.S. investors at $6.4 billion as of 1983.[14] Although it is now illegal for U.S. citizens to purchase shares issued after October 1986, it is still possible for risk-taking investors to purchase American Depository Receipts (ADRs) of South African companies like Anglo-American Corporation and De Beers. These ADRs had doubled in value in the nine months ending in May 1987.[15]

International bank lending is the critical third category of foreign investment. As of December 1986, U.S. banks had $2.96 billion in outstanding loans to South Africa. Of this amount, about two-thirds was owed by South African banks and the rest by private and public sector borrowers. Canadian bank loans probably do not exceed $150 million (Canadian) as of 1986.[16]

Money and micro-chips

When South Africa enters a period of economic and political crisis, foreign exchange becomes a key issue. Historically, foreign lenders have been crucial in bailing out South Africa after the Sharpeville crisis of 1960 (see Chapter Two), during the period from 1974 to 1977 and once again in 1981 and '82 when the country faced a current account crisis* and a later unprecedented political uprising. In this latest crisis, international bankers such as Chase Manhattan declared a moratorium on lending to the South African government. Shortly afterward, the Reagan administration banned such loans by executive order. U.S. law now prohibits most new loans. (Citibank, Barclays and other large banks have sold their banking interests in South Africa to local capital.) Nevertheless, the leniency shown to South Africa concerning repayment after it declared a moratorium on paying debts tends to confirm the apartheid rulers' confidence that bankers are more interested in the stability of a government than in the morality of its policy.[17]

Foreign investment has played a key role in financing gov-

---

* Current, as opposed to capital, account refers to current trading balances—merchandise imported and exported, gold output and other "current items."

ernment expenses in the strategic areas of defense, balance of payments and imports of sophisticated machines and equipment.[18] Foreign capital comes not only in the form of money but also as technology, expertise and equipment. In a 1973 survey, three-quarters of the manufacturing firms interviewed said that 90 percent of their technology was imported.

One example of South Africa's dependence on imports for technology is in the field of computers. United States computer companies have tended to dominate this South African market. In 1985, IBM controlled 40 percent of the installed business computers and 20 percent of the overall market. About 17 percent of its business was with the government. IBM computers have been used to process military payrolls and to help apartheid keep track of population records. IBM is not the only company involved:

> Advanced computers licensed for sale by the U.S. government have played a key role in Pretoria's ability to manage the African, "Coloured," Asian and Indian populations. . . . U.S. companies such as NCR Corporation, Control Data, IBM, Burroughs and Sperry have outfitted other agencies including the Department of the Prime Minister, Department of Statistics and a large number of local government bodies that serve as administrative shock troops of the apartheid system.[19]

While President Reagan has banned computer sales to the South African military and police, sales to private firms and to other government agencies are still legal. And although IBM has now announced that it is "withdrawing" from South Africa, it has set up a new corporate arrangement with its employees. IBM expects to get credit for disinvesting while continuing to sell, distribute and service its products in South Africa.[20]

Energy know-how

American technical expertise is also of particular value to South Africa in the field of energy. The co-author of a recent study of foreign investment in South Africa has made this assessment:

> While many of these U.S. firms have to be considered important cogs in the South African economy, perhaps none have a more vital, even strategic role than the U.S. oil companies there: Chevron . . . , Exxon, Mobil, Phillips, The Standard Oil Company of Ohio (SOHIO) and Texaco.[21]

Chevron and Texaco own one large refinery near Cape Town and Mobil operates one near Durban. Together they process 40 percent of all crude oil coming into the country. Fluor Corporation, an engineering firm, has been the managing partner of synthetic fuel installations that turn South Africa's abundant coal into liquid petroleum. A Fluor subsidiary has maintained the important nuclear power station at Koeberg on the Cape. But in 1986 Fluor claimed that it had sold its South African subsidiaries' assets to a European trust company in response to a threat by the City of Los Angeles to deny construction contracts to Fluor if it did not cease doing business in South Africa.[22]

Investment for whose benefit?

Foreign investments, exports of minerals, and imports of money and technology are what make the apartheid regime strong and seemingly invincible. During the heyday of apartheid's prosperity from 1964 to 1973, investors were able to earn 16 percent or more when the normal return in other places was 12 percent.[23] Today those profits have been exposed to public view and denounced as based on a racist exploitation of labor. A worldwide campaign against apartheid and in favor of sanctions has raised issues of conscience for a segment of the international investment community. Unless that pressure continues, investors and traders will go on with their profitable investments.

While a strong economy is a precondition of prosperity, there is no evidence that the investments, trade and technology South Africa has imported and the West has exported to it have helped raise the standard of living of most South Africans, who continue to live in conditions like those of the most impoverished nations. Nor have they done anything to bring about political rights for the majority of the population. Small wonder, then, that the resistance to apartheid within South Africa has called for comprehensive trade and investment sanctions. Sanctions operate on the assumption that South Africa is not self-sufficient; we have seen that that assumption is indeed based on economic reality. To take away one of the legs of the apartheid stool, making it unstable, can promote the change of heart that could lead to negotiations with the legitimate leaders of the black majority and produce a democratic and non-racist society. In Chapter Nine, we shall consider the details of the argument for sanctions.

Chapter Six:
No Easy Walk to Freedom

In this chapter we will examine the strength of the resistance to apartheid by South Africans themselves. The most important single voice of that resistance continues to be the African National Congress, even though as a banned organization it must operate underground, from exile or even from prison. A related form of resistance, which we will call "Africanist," defines resistance primarily in terms that exclude white participation. In addition, legal and open forms of resistance are carried on by groups that include trade unions, broad democratic coalitions formed around specific issues and local community organizing.

The most famous of the ANC leaders, Nelson Mandela, once described the kind of commitment that resistance requires:

> You can see that "there is no easy walk to freedom anywhere and many of us will have to pass through the valley of the shadow of death again and again before we reach the mountain-tops of our desires." Dangers and difficulties have not deterred us in the past; they will not frighten us now. But we must be prepared for them like [men and women] who mean business and who do not waste energy in vain talk and idle action. The way of preparation for action lies in our rooting out all impurity and indiscipline from our organization and making it the bright and shining instrument that will cleave its way to Africa's freedom.[1]

When he wrote these words in 1953, Nelson Mandela could not have known their full significance. The organization he referred to, the African National Congress, was entering a phase of new and vigorous protest against apartheid, but those were "the early days."

Today (in 1987), Nelson Mandela is sixty-nine; he has spent the last twenty-three years in prison. Yet Mandela in prison is more influential than ever before, because he is the symbol of national resistance. And the ANC, illegal though it is, commands the loyalty of more South Africans than any other organization.

South Africa has offered Mandela his freedom provided he and his organization repudiate the use of arms in their struggle. But Mandela has refused this offer if it means putting ANC at a critical disadvantage. Mandela put it this way:

> I am suprised at the conditions that the government wants to impose on me. I am not a violent man. My colleagues and I wrote to Malan [Prime Minister, 1948-54] asking for a round-table conference to find a solution to the problems of our country, but that was ignored. When Strijdom [Prime Minister, 1954-58] was in power, we made the same offer. Again it was ignored. When Verwoerd [Prime Minister, 1958-66] was in power, we asked for a national convention for all the people in South Africa to decide on their future. This, too, was in vain.
>
> Let Botha [the present State President] show he is different. . . . Let him renounce violence. Let him say that he will dismantle apartheid. Let him unban the people's organization, the African National Congress. Let him free all who have been imprisoned, banished or exiled for their opposition to apartheid.
>
> What freedom am I offered while the organization of the people remains banned? What freedom am I being offered when I may be arrested on a past offense? . . . What freedom am I offered when I must ask for permission to live in an urban area? . . . Only free [people] can negotiate. Prisoners cannot enter into contracts. . . . [Nelson Mandela's reply, read by his daughter Zinzi at a public rally in Soweto, February 10, 1985][2]

By the time Mandela made this statement, the African National Congress had become the leading force in what it and others saw as a revolutionary process gathering momentum and force. Yet the ANC was still in exile; in South Africa itself, it was an illegal, underground organization.

Today the gold, green and black colors of ANC, banned as it is, are displayed openly and vigorously at public rallies and at funerals for those killed by the police. From thousands of throats the ANC's rallying cry, AMANDLA! (Power!) AWETHU! (It shall be ours!) is openly, defiantly shouted across the land. Several surveys have shown that the ANC has the support of a majority of urban blacks and that Nelson Mandela would easily win any parliamentary election for the presidency of South Africa if such an election were held.

In township after township, African youth have organized a kind of urban guerilla warfare of their own, following the general guidelines of the ANC's call to make South Africa ungovernable and to make a peoples' war on the apartheid regime. Ironically, these tactics are now being criticized as "brutal" and "violent" by a South African government that for decade upon decade has used indiscriminate violence against defenseless civilians.

With its leaders in jail, the struggle goes on and continues to be well-led and comparatively well-disciplined in spite of the violence visited on the people. In almost every African township, the people themselves have created their own forms of mass organization and government.

Let us now look in more detail at the organization and aims of the African National Congress, the other South African liberation movements and other forms of resistance.

The African National Congress

Established in 1912, the ANC was a major beneficiary of the upsurge of black revolt which began with the Soweto uprising of 1976. The bravery of this generation of students, facing tanks with rocks and bottles, caught the imagination of their elders and the world. Tom Lodge, a South African political scientist, remarks that while the students lacked political acumen, ". . . the effects of the uprising were to stimulate a generalisation of resistance movements amongst Africans in South Africa."[3]

Soweto marked not only a change from relative quiet to broad, militant resistance but also the exodus from South Africa of several thousand student activists, who fled into exile to take up arms against apartheid. Not all of these exiles went into guerilla warfare training but by 1978, according to South African intelligence estimates, some four thousand were in training in Angola, Tanzania or Libya, most of them under ANC auspices.[4] By 1986 the ANC was said to have six to ten thousand military trainees in Angola or Eastern Europe.[5]

While some exiles sought out the training camps and offices of the Pan-Africanist Congress (see page 37) or tried to build their own liberation army, the vast majority ended up with the African National Congress, finding that it had better international support, a clear political strategy and organizational coherence.

The ANC's political philosophy

The ANC is not a political party; it is a national liberation movement comprising a variety of political points of view with an agreed-upon platform set out in the Freedom Charter (see study guide, *Until We Are Free.*) Reading it, one can see that it is a populist manifesto, which might be compared to the Peoples' Party (Populist) platform adopted in 1892 at a convention held in Omaha, Nebraska, or to similar documents adopted in Canada or in Great Britain by parties representing working class people. The Charter is not a communist document. It does not, for example, call for immediate or complete nationalization of all means of production or for the establishment of a dictatorship of the proletariat. It does include guarantees of freedoms while calling for public control and ownership of monopolies and banks.

Membership in the ANC has been open to all races since 1969, and since 1985 its National Executive has also been multi-racial, although the great majority of the members and officers are African.

As we have pointed out in Chapter Three, the earliest leaders of ANC were deeply influenced by Christian beliefs and Western values. Many current members of the ANC are church people or have been brought up in the church: the Mandela family is a prominent example.

The ANC's relationship with the Communist Party is a bone of contention in the United States, especially in political circles. Some would argue, for example, that the ANC is so dominated by the South African Communist Party and is so beholden to the Soviet Union that the United States government should not even speak to ANC leaders.

This point of view is not widely shared in Africa. African people have endured centuries of slavery, colonialism and imperialist exploitation initated by European and North American countries. They are therefore apt to see Western capitalist states and enterprises not as kind-hearted but rather as greedy and powerful and unprincipled. Marxist theory is generally seen as a helpful tool in understanding how capitalism has worked to Africa's detriment. In 1964 Nelson Mandela described to the court that sentenced him his own search for a viable political philosophy:

> Today I am attracted by the idea of a classless society, an
> attraction which springs in part from Marxist reading and,

Government orders to use Afrikaans in schools sparked student demonstrations in Soweto in 1976.

Peter Magubane

Cedric Nunn/Afrapix

Outside a Durban prison, the mother of a child detained during 1986 talks with a Black Sash member.

At a Kruger Day celebration in the Orange Free State, Afrikaner children sit in front of a monument commemorating the Great Trek of the 1830s.

Africans have long counted on nonviolent protest to change South African laws and attitudes. When government forces repel peaceful though angry demonstrators with violence (as in student protests, right), marches end in funerals (below). In turn, funerals become new demonstrations against apartheid as well as expressions of grief and faith. And the police (above) keep vigilant eyes on all gatherings.

Photos on these pages by Peter Magubane

Washing clothes in the black township of Zwelitemba outside Worcester in the Cape Province. The shortage of housing and services for Africans is acute in urban locations as well as in the "homelands."

Many black women work as domestic servants for white families, as does this woman at Sun City. Caring for their employers' children often entails days or weeks of separation from their own children.

in part, from my admiration for the structure and organization of early African societies in this country. . . .

It is true. . . that I have been influenced by Marxist thought. But this is also true of many of the leaders of the new independent States. Such widely different persons as Gandhi, Nehru, Nkrumah and Nasser all acknowledge this fact. We all accept the need for some form of socialism to enable our people to catch up with the advanced countries of this world and to overcome their legacy of extreme poverty. But this does not mean we are Marxists. . . .

From my reading of Marxist literature and from conversations with Marxists, I have gained the impression that communists regard the parliamentary system of the West as undemocratic and reactionary. But, on the contrary, I am an admirer of such a system. . . .

I have great respect for British political institutions and for the country's system of justice. I regard the British Parliament as the most democratic institution in the world, and the independence and impartiality of its judiciary never fail to arouse my admiration.

The American Congress, that country's doctrine of separation of powers, as well as the independence of its judiciary, arouses in me similar sentiments.[6]

Nelson Mandela and his former law partner, Oliver Tambo, are still widely regarded as non-Communist, pragmatic nationalists rather than as Marxist ideologists. They are widely respected middle-class professional people who are representative of the older generation of the ANC leadership. They are regarded as "moderates," but they never separate themselves from the whole of the ANC nor do they wish to see it divided by such labels.

Refusal to pick apart an alliance

It is also clear, however, that the African National Congress has had a close and cordial relationship with the South African Communist Party (SACP). This relationship is considered vital to its alliance of forces. One key to the gratitude the ANC feels toward the Communist Party is the fact that for decades it was the only party in South Africa that supported equal rights for all South Africans.[7]

Communists within the ANC alliance accept the Freedom Charter as the primary document outlining the first phase of what is for them a two-stage revolution: first, national liberation is to be achieved; then South Africa will be transformed into an egalitarian society through the victory of the working class. Given the great difficulties that Mozambique, Angola and Zimbabwe—each led by a Marxist-Leninist party—have experienced in moving from phase one to phase two, South African Communist Party leaders are reluctant to promise to move fast or undemocratically toward the second phase.

Although the ANC has been criticized from the left by some intellectuals as insufficiently rooted in the working class,[8] there can be little doubt that the ANC is an organization of the political left in which Communists play a strong role. ANC leadership would also admit that their years of exile and the actions of the government have left the organization with a weaker relationship to working class movements than they would like. Because leaders of the ANC-related South African Congress of Trade Unions (SACTU) have been so effectively banned, detained and jailed, the ANC has not been able openly to help organize working class Africans. Nevertheless, ANC influence remains strong in trade union circles. At its second annual conference in July 1987, the Congress of South African Trade Unions (COSATU) recognized the Freedom Charter as its guiding document and called on the government to lift its ban on the ANC.[9]

Responding to a recent directive from Congress, the U.S. State Department has released a study alleging that half of the thirty members of the National Executive, the ANC governing body, are "known or suspected SACP members." But Thomas Karis, an American expert on black politics in South Africa, states that only three individuals can be demonstrated conclusively to be Communist Party members. The South African government contends that twenty-three of these thirty leaders are SACP members. Obviously, no one can know for certain, and suspicion is not evidence. In any case, the ANC has refused to be drawn into making distinctions between members who are Communists and those who are not. To do so, they reason, would cause divisive splits and lead to the kind of witch-hunt that marked the U.S. in the McCarthy era of the 1950s.

Another reason for ANC's reluctance to distinguish its Communist membership is the need to protect itself against inquisition. As Joe Slovo, the Secretary General of SACP and the first white member of the ANC National Executive, said recently: "We [the SACP] are an illegal, underground organization and we do not name our members."[10]

The ANC and the Soviet Union

Liberation movements are not in a position to choose who will aid them. They go as supplicants, asking various countries for help with what they need. Like many African liberation movements, the ANC has not found the United States supportive even in humanitarian, non-military concerns.

Oliver Tambo, the current ANC president, remembers his early experiences in seeking help in the struggle against apartheid:

> It was in the United States that I went first [in the early 1960s] to ask for assistance and to address meetings addressing Americans, asking them for support. But we received no real response. . . .
>
> We were fascinated by the history of the United States. . . . And we thought if there was any country which would understand our position, it was the United States. There was the South, there was the Civil War, and then there was the civil rights movement. There were laws against racism, which they enforce. It is the opposite in South Africa—the laws dictate racism, they punish people who are not racists. . . .
>
> I only went to the Soviet Union in 1963, and when I got there, in the first instance, I said we needed some funds. They gave us some. I'd never handled so much money before—it was only $20,000. I went to China after that, and they gave us money.[11]

A recent example of the United States' approach to the ANC is the sanctions legislation adopted by Congress in 1986. The Comprehensive Anti-Apartheid Act explicitly opposes any form of armed resistance to apartheid, calling on the ANC to give up "terrorism" and "violence" and to agree to open negotiations with the South African authorities. In view of the U.S.'s funding of the rebels in Afghanistan, the contras in Nicaragua and the UNITA movement in Angola, it is clear that its position does not stem from an opposition to the use of force or violence as such. Rather, it is based on a generic opposition to "communism."

From experience, the ANC has learned that it cannot look to the U.S. for any kind of help, military or non-military. When in the United States, ANC people are often threatened with deportation, denied visas or barred from visiting parts of the country. As one older ANC member recently told an interviewer: "If we want to go to Moscow, they will meet us at the airport. If we want to go to New York, we will have to beg for a visa, if we get one at all. A lot of it is as simple as that."[12]

Although the Soviet Union and Eastern Europe are major sources of military equipment and training and of scholarships for study in Europe, they are not the sole suppliers of aid to the ANC. The Organization of African Unity, Scandinavian countries and many small non-communist countries such as Austria and the Netherlands have also been helpful in supplying financial and material assistance for such non-military projects as schools, refugee settlements and model farming cooperatives for ANC exiles in Zambia, Tanzania and Angola.

On the abandonment of guerilla warfare

Armed violence is by no means the most important facet of the ANC's strength. Broad political campaigns, consumer boycotts, trade union struggles and other essentially nonviolent methods are equally, if not more, important. The ANC belives that if effective and comprehensive international sanctions against South Africa were adopted, violence and suffering would be reduced because the government would be pressured to achieve meaningful negotiations sooner. However, because of the apartheid state's use of violence, its belief in military toughness and its philosophy that ruthless force used unsparingly and relentlessly will maintain its power, the ANC is in no position to abandon armed force as a counter-method. It sees its use of arms as a self-defense measure to protect the people themselves and as a way of achieving some measure of people's power.

Joe Slovo, who is chief of staff of the ANC military wing, *Umkhonto we Sizwe*, put the issue this way: "Abandon this weapon prematurely, and you abandon the struggle. You leave them with no worries. It has got to be intensified."[13] According to Oliver Tambo, "It is only through the intensification of the struggle that Botha will see the need for serious negotiations."[14]

Negotiations

To people of good will it often seems that the issue of apartheid could be settled through negotiations. But to rectify such a grossly unequal situation would require that those with wealth, status and power choose to make sacrifices. This they simply are not prepared to do. In fact, it may be that only a prospect of worse consequences—the doom of the society, the deaths of whites and severe damage to their property interests—could compel negotiations that are politically unpalatable at present.[15]

The 1986 visit to South Africa of the Commonwealth Eminent Persons Group, who are moderates eager to promote dialogue, confirms this view:

> . . . while the Government claims to be ready to negotiate, it is in truth not yet prepared to negotiate fundamental change, nor to countenance the creation of genuine democratic structures, nor to face the prospect of the end of white domination and white power in the foreseeable future. Its programme of reform does not end apartheid, but seeks to give it a less inhuman face.[16]

The present state of guerilla attacks

Because the government censors news related to security issues and because the ANC is equally cautious, the extent of ANC guerilla operations cannot be accurately known. In recent years, however, the ANC has made a number of spectacular attacks on large and strategic objectives. In June 1980 the ANC set fire to two SASOL oil-from-coal plants; in December 1982 the Koeberg nuclear power station was attacked. In May 1983, the headquarters of the South African Air Force in Pretoria was car-bombed.

Recent attacks have been more frequent but their targets are relatively less conspicuous. Urban guerilla warfare continues in the African townships, which remain occupied by the South African military. African collaborators, informers and police agents are dealt with in ways that may seem brutal to outsiders. The ANC discourages "necklacing" of "sellouts" (collaborators with the apartheid government) and prefers their political isolation instead. Yet "necklacing" does happen, and the ANC understands it to be a reaction to the government's violence.[17] (The ANC hopes to guide the conflict but cannot always control it.)

Outside the cities, ANC guerillas are beginning to attack outlying white farms by planting land mines on farm roads in the northern Transvaal. One reason for doing this, according to the ANC, is that white farms are actually South Africa's "first line of defense." Joe Modise, the guerilla army commander, stated the rationale:

Naturally, when we say [we are] taking the war to the white areas, we do not mean we are going to look for civilians. We are going to look for the very people who are enforcing these racist laws.

These farmers along the border have been organized into military formations and their main task, really, is to deal with us, to inform on us, to confront us when they feel strong enough to do so. Hence they are trained, and their wives and children.[18]

Because of intense South African pressure on neighboring black independent countries, establishing bases in adjacent countries is no longer possible for the ANC—as it once was for the liberation movements of Mozambique, Angola and Zimbabwe. Instead, the ANC has to rely on bases inside South Africa.

The "Africanist" resistance

During the days following World War II when ANC leaders like Mandela and Tambo were rising to prominence, a powerful new stream of thinking emerged within the ranks of the ANC's Youth League. This ideology came to be known as "Africanist" and the group within ANC who initiated it to be called the "Africanists." They were inspired by Anton M. Lembede, a charismatic leader who called for an end to collaboration with the oppressor and for a recovery of African socialism and democratic practices. The Africanists drew on a long tradition of Pan-Africanism which existed in the United States and Europe as well as in Africa.

The Africanists argued that the Freedom Charter conceded too much to whites when it said that the land did not belong to black Africans only but to all who lived in South Africa. The land had been stolen, Africanists held, and the thieves should not be rewarded:

The African people have an inalienable claim on every inch of the African soil. In the memory of humanity as a whole, this continent has been the homelands of Africans. . . . The non-Africans are guests of the Africans. . . . [and] have to adjust themselves to the interests of Africa, their new home.[19]

Nor did Africanists want to collaborate with avowed communists, whom they saw as importers of a European philosophy. Instead of a multiracial liberalism (which the Charter could be said to exemplify) or Marxism, Africanists advocated consolidating

African people into a massive, solid resistance. This would require, above all, the psychological liberation of blacks.

Those in the ANC who opposed the Africanists were called "Charterists," because they stood by the Freedom Charter. They believed the Africanists were creating a kind of Afrikaner nationalism in reverse. If Africanists were so fearful of the movement being dominated by the relatively small number of whites who oppose appartheid, they had hardly achieved the liberation of consciousness they advocated.

In 1959 the Africanists broke away from ANC altogether and formed the Pan-Africanist Congress of Azania (PAC) under the leadership of Robert Sobukwe. It was PAC which organized the nonviolent campaign against passes that culminated in the Sharpeville incident of March 21, 1960.

After Sharpeville, an offshoot of PAC, called POQO, used terrorism and murder to create a wave of incidents in the western Cape and the Transkei. (POQO was short for the Xhosa phrase, Um Afrika Poqo, meaning "Africans Alone!" the central principle of PAC organizing.) By 1963 the police had stopped it by arresting over 3,000 alleged members.

In following years PAC tried—not very sucessfully—to mount an armed guerilla movement. After the 1977 arrest of what seemed to be its entire underground structure, divisions arose between its military and political leaders, followed by bitter factional struggles. Since 1981 some measure of unity has been restored.[20]

While the Organization of African Unity has recognized both ANC and PAC as legitimate liberation movements, there can be little doubt that PAC is by far the weaker organization.[21]

Black Consciousness

The Africanist stream of thought re-emerged within South Africa during the late 1960s among students at the various black educational institutions. These students had not only been influenced by the Pan-Africanist tradition, but had also read Stokely Carmichael, H. Rap Brown, George Jackson, Malcolm X, James Cone and other advocates of black power from the United States.

In 1968 the South African Students Organization (SASO) was formed, breaking with the National Student Organization. Steve Biko, SASO's leader, wrote of the need to liberate blacks from psychological domination by whites—especially white liberals:

The philosophy of Black Conciousness . . . expresses group
pride and the determination by the blacks to rise and attain
the envisaged self. At the heart of this kind of thinking is
the realization by the blacks that the most potent weapon
in the hands of the oppressor is the mind of the oppressed. . . .

The myth of integration as propounded under the banner
of the liberal ideology must be cracked because it makes
people believe that something is being achieved when in
reality the artificially integrated circles are a soporific to the
blacks while salving the consciences of the few guilt-striken
whites.[22]

With the slogan that blacks must "go it alone," various black
organizations began to grow; they united in the Black Peoples
Convention. A Black Allied Workers Union was formed. An Inter-
denominational African Ministers Alliance was part of the new
stream of Black Consciousness. Within the churches, black caucuses
began to develop a black theology.

The Black Consciousness movement criticized both the ANC
and the PAC for moving to political confrontation before changing
the consciousness of black people: the first order of business should
be to develop among blacks a sense of solidarity; thus the dignity
and collective strength of the African people would be built up.

The Black Consciousness movement received an enormous boost
from the student-led uprising of June 16, 1976. In its wake, more
Black Consciousness projects began to arise.

It was not capitalism nor scientific socialism but "black communalism" that would create the new society. Black communalism
focussed on small, community-directed projects. To demonstrate
this concept, students became involved in community health
clinics and other enterprises. Black Consciousness did not define
an overall economic structure, so it was often difficult to see how
to adapt traditional African communal ownership to a highly
industrialized society that emphasized technical skills.

The Soweto uprising of 1976 showed that Black Consciousness
was a powerful force that could mobilize real resistance to apartheid. The South African government did not wait to see how the
Black Consciousness movement might develop. It rounded up Biko
and other leaders of the movement and held them in detention.
Then, shockingly, Biko died in detention, killed by inhumane
treatment and gross negligence by police doctors. Biko became

a martyr whose death gave new determination and depth to the whole resistance movement.

In October 1977 all Black Consciousness movement organizations were banned. The Christian Institute, the supportive church organization described in Chapter Three, was banned then as well.[23]

Successors to the Africanist tradition

The Azanian Peoples' Organization, AZAPO, was created in 1978 to carry on the Black Consciousness tradition. AZAPO contends that no South African political movement can be integrated, because integration assumes an equality denied by the privileges granted to whites. It was AZAPO that launched the National Forum, a coalition of black organizations, to combat the South African government's new constitution (see page 61).

In recent years, AZAPO's emphasis has shifted from issues of race toward those of class. A recent study commissioned by the South African Council of Churches defines the shift in this way:

What is clear is that those who subscribe today to an Africanist philosophy within AZAPO and NF [National Forum] are using an explicit class analysis, and identify the root problem in South Africa not as racialism but racial capitalism.

AZAPO's policy extends the black consciousness philosophy in two ways. Firstly, it recognizes that some blacks collaborate with the system. . . . "Black" therefore means "oppressed," yet some blacks belong to the "oppressor" class. Secondly, it insists on the importance of the trade union "as an instrument that can bring about the redistribution of power." Despite this assertion, AZAPO does not appear to have formal links with significant labour organizations.[24]

An even more radical shift in thinking has taken place in the student organizations that have inherited the tradition of the South African Student Organization (SASO). The Azanian Students' Organization (AZASO) and the Congress of South African Students (COSAS), founded in 1979 but recently banned, both recognize the need for blacks and whites to work together:

The struggle knows no colour. The enemy is neither black nor white. This means the solution will never simply be a black government. . . . We must work together towards a free, democratic and non-racial South Africa. [Wantu Zanzile, COSAS President, 1982][25]

Trade unions

Another major force of resistance is the growing strength of democratic, non-racial trade unionism.

We saw in Chapter Two that one aim of the apartheid policy makers was to smash the African labor movement. The great bulk of Africans who worked in industry and commerce had been excluded by law from the provisions of the Industrial Conciliation Act of 1924. In 1956 the apartheid government strengthened the law to exclude "Natives" totally. Their unions, deemed fraternal associations, were not allowed to strike or to bargain collectively through the government-sanctioned process, which was used primarily by white labor. That whole situation has now changed.

In 1972 and '73 a spontaneous upsurge of strikes by African workers in Durban and in Namibia heralded a new phase of labor militancy. This upsurge has by no means ended. Today, more than two million workers are union members out of a total labor force of some ten million. Roughly half of that two million are organized African trade unionists.

It is important to know that South African trade unions are divided into two main categories:

1. Unions that represent a privileged minority of the labor force, which historically have tried to preserve color bars. These unions have largely been composed of whites, with very small numbers of skilled "Coloureds" and "Indians." These unions have also had "parallel" African affiliates, whose membership is perhaps a quarter of the white unions. The confederation of these unions is the Trade Union Congress of South Africa (TUCSA). In recent years the influence and membership of this category of unions have declined.

2. Unions that are non-racist and democratic in their constitution and life. These unions are primarily composed of African workers at all levels. Most of them are open to all workers irrespective of race; in some cases they include whites.

Non-racist, democratic unions are steadily growing in power, influence and membership. Could such a vibrant, growing trade union movement be a political force as well? Could it overturn apartheid or collaborate with other forces to do so?

Such questions obviously concern the government. When a new wave of spontaneous strike activity began in 1972, the government, under pressure from employers, initiated what are called the Wiehahn reforms. These measures attempted to provide a regular, legal channel through which black trade unions could be registered and regulated. By regulation, the government intended to prevent unions from engaging in political activities which would rock the stability of the apartheid state. At the same time, a channel for negotiating purely economic issues could avoid strikes. At first, African unions were hesitant to accept registration, seeing it as a dubious "gift," fearing that it meant submission to white control. Today that fear has subsided. Because of the size and strength of the labor movement, registration is no longer seen as an absolute bar to political work, and most unions have accepted registration as a legitimate tactic in organizing against apartheid.

Trade union issues remain

Should the democratic trade unions be open to all or should they be exclusively for blacks? Those that could be called "Black Consciousness" unions, which comprise 100,000 to 150,000 members, give the second answer. They are grouped in two federations, the Council of Unions of South Africa (CUSA) and the Azanian Confederation of Trade Unions.

The first answer, however, is given by a much larger grouping, the Confederation of South African Trade Unions (COSATU), which embraces 33 of the largest unions and claims more than 700,000 paid members. Formed in November 1985, COSATU represents the culmination of five years of intense negotiation. One of its principal aims is to help build a "united working class movement regardless of "race, colour, creed or sex."

How should trade unions respond to political issues regarding the abolition of apartheid? Should they take up community struggles or confine themselves to more immediate economic concerns such as wages and factory conditions? These questions have no easy answers. Workers know well how easily management and the government can replace those who strike or send "troublemakers" back to the bantustans.

Nevertheless, the trade union movement as a whole has moved toward a much more openly political position. Although most strikes are over such issues as union recognition, wages, dismissals or cutbacks in the labor force, increasingly the strikes have had political dimensions. Moreover, the working class movement increasingly has been willing to engage in brief stay-at-home or general strikes to call for the abolition of the present racist order.[26]

In November 1984, 800,00 workers stayed at home for two days. On May 1, 1986, 1.5 million workers responded to COSATU's call to stay at home in support of demands that May Day become a national holiday. And on June 16 of that year, the anniversary of the Soweto uprising, the power of South Africas black workers was shown even more dramatically:

> Buses rode empty, shops stood shuttered and urban workplaces fell silent as millions of blacks stolidly withheld their labor and patronage. . . . None of President P.W. Botha's emergency decrees could prevent the impressive protest. . . . The oppressed not only shamed their oppressors, they struck where even racists feel pain, at the purse.[27]

The thinking behind COSATU's actions was outlined by Cyril Ramaphosa of the National Union of Mineworkers:

> Workers' political strength depends upon building strong and militant organization in the workplace. It is also important to draw people into a programme for the restructuring of society in order to make sure that the wealth of our society is democratically controlled and shared by its people. It is important to realise that the political struggle is not only to remove the government. We must also eliminate unemployment, improve education, improve health facilities and the wealth of the society must be shared among all those that work in this country. . . . We all agree that the struggle of workers on the shop floor cannot be separated from the wider struggle for liberation.[28]

Coalitions form around specific issues

United Democratic Front and National Forum

When in 1983 the government enacted the latest and most ambitious of its cosmetic reforms, a new constitution creating a Tricameral Parliament, it could hardly have anticipated the breadth and strength of the opposition to this "new dispensation." While whites overwhelmingly voted in favor of the new constitution, 80 percent of the "Indian" and "Coloured" population refused to vote—even though the reform was supposed to give them a greater share in government. The black majority, 70 percent of the population, which is not allowed to vote at all, was totally excluded from any meaningful political power by the proposed constitution.

Two organizations sprang into existence to oppose the alleged "reform." The largest of these was the United Democratic Front (UDF), a coalition of some 600 groups. It was led by many activists associated with the ANC: Oscar Mpetha, Archie Gumede and Albertina Sisulu. UDF deliberately sought to bring in people of all races. Its groups ranged from Black Sash (an organization primarily of white middle-class women) to the student radicals of the Congress of South African Students. Its honorary advisors[*] included Nelson Mandela, Walter Sisulu and Govan Mbeki[†], the top ANC leaders of the 1960s, who are still in prison. Another such advisor was Allan Boesak, the outstanding theologian and leader of the Dutch Reformed Sendingkerk. UDF called for a united, democratic South Africa based on the will of the people as a whole. The formation of UDF was seen as a reaffirmation of the Freedom Charter's principles, even though agreement with the charter was not a precondition for joining.

The South African government found the UDF intentions treasonable and charged sixteen prominent leaders with attempting to overthrow the government. In the cases tried so far, the courts pronounced these charges unfounded, as they had in the 1955 trials. Nevertheless, UDF activists have gone into hiding because of the government's sweeping use of detention without trial under its Declaration of State of Emergency. Over 70 percent of recent government attacks and detentions have been aimed at leaders and members of UDF organizations. On October 9, 1986, UDF was declared an "Affected Organization," which means it can no longer receive funds from overseas. It will be no surprise if next the government declares it a banned organization.

The second coalition to arise in opposition to the proposed constitution was The National Forum. Initiated by AZAPO, the Black Conciousness organization, it was composed of more than 200 black organizations, with particular emphasis on anti-racism. The N.F. manifesto called for a democratic and anti-racist republic "where the interests of the workers shall be paramount. . .[29]"

While there are differences between the UDF and the N.F., there are also points of agreement:

- The government is deceitful and untrustworthy, a past master at double-speak and double-think.

---

[*] The UDF lists these leaders as "patrons."
[†] Govan Mbeki was released in November 1987

- The reforms were cosmetic, designed to fool the world while preserving rule by a white clique.
- Apartheid must be abolished, not reformed.
- Negotiations have to start from a principle of non-racism.
- The government must commit itself to end apartheid, pull its troops out of the townships, create conditions of political freedom for all parties and release all political prisoners.
- Negotiations must be held only with those who have authority and standing to speak on behalf of the people.[30]

Community organizations and civic associations

In most African townships, government-sponsored "councils" have ceased to exist. Government-sponsored councillors have been forced to resign, put under a state of siege by popular forces, or simply disappeared. In many parts of the country, newly organized street, block and areas committees have in effect taken over control of the townships. In the eastern Cape townships, well-developed organizations based on popular democracy have been at work for some time.

These township organizations have launched a variety of nonviolent boycotts and other pressure campaigns. Township residents, for example, have refused to pay rent or utility bills to protest the high cost of living. In Soweto, the boycott has produced a 30 million Rand deficit in the governmental authority's account. Boycotts of buses and of white businesses have been carried on, particularly in the urban areas of the eastern Cape.[31]

Support for detainees

The Detainees' Parents Support Committee (DPSC) was formed to meet an urgent need for information on what is happening to children and other family members swept up and imprisoned by the South African authorities. Under the State of Emergency declared on June 12, 1986, little or no information could be published about who had been picked up, who was being held or who had been released. Working with churches and others, the DPSC tries to piece together what information does exist and to expose the scandalously large number of children who have been detained without trial.

The National Medical and Dental Association (NAMDA) provides free medical examinations to ex-detainees. NAMDA has accused many medical colleagues of ignoring the detainees' physical signs of torture. A recent NAMDA study showed that 72 percent of the ex-detainees examined had been physically assaulted, 89 percent beaten and 25 percent suffocated.

The End Conscription Campaign

As the South African government confronts its neighboring nations (which are independent and black-governed) and the growing, determined struggle against apartheid within its borders, it relies more and more on its military to maintain control. So when conscripted, young white men are likely to face military duties in the African townships as well as in Namibia and Angola. The prospect of being ordered to shoot black Africans, break up church meetings with tear gas and endure the hostility that an army of occupation faces can make apartheid real to the young conscience in a way that news headlines may not. Conscription is mandatory for all white male citizens; conscientious objection to military service requires an absolutely pacifist position based on theology. So many whites who resist apartheid on other grounds are slipping out of the country or otherwise evading military service. Over 7,000 are estimated to have failed to turn up for military duty in the call-up of January 1985, compared to 1,600 for all of 1984.[32]

The End Conscription Campaign (ECC) arose to protest the militarization of South Africa and to awaken the consciences of those who face conscription, helping them explore the possibility of refusing to cooperate with the draft. The ECC is supported by some South African churches; in 1985 ECC sponsored a three-week period of public vigil, prayer and fasting. More recently it has promoted a campaign to get troops out of the townships. The story of Carl Niehaus in Chapter One illustrates how a growing number of young whites feel about military service.

Youth and Education

The National Education Crisis Committee was born in 1985 in response to the chaotic state of education. For four years, black students had been boycotting schools to protest the inferior education they receive. But young people still need education. The NEEC attempted to discuss curriculum and other issues with the Department of Education. The results were uniformly negative. The Department of Education took a hard line; soon all but one of the NEEC leadership had been detained.

In September 1986, students boycotted schools as a protest against the presence of military in educational institutions and against the large numbers of student detentions. Thousands burned the new identification cards (replacing passes) which the government has required as a part of its crackdown.

On March 28, 1987, a new organization called the South African Youth Congress (SAYCO) was launched at Cape Town. SAYCO claimed to represent 500,000 to 700,000 students organized in 1,000 local youth affiliates. Like the Congress of South African Students, which had been banned, its purpose is to unify and give political direction to all sectors of youth—workers, students and the unemployed, regardless of race, color, sex or religion. Its 25-year-old president, Peter Mokoba, has been in and out of detention and prison for 10 years. Three other officers have also been detained.

Summing it up

Since July 1985 the government has been ruling primarily by the use of police-state powers, by military rule in the townships, by stepped-up detentions and by unprecedented manipulation of information, censoring all news and completely stopping publication of some. These efforts clearly have not succeeded in re-establishing the government's authority.

Continuing use of brute force shows that the government has no other way to rule. Its authority is not legitimate in the eyes of the majority of the people. Although the heady days when open defiance seemed ready to overturn apartheid are gone, the resistance has not been broken in spite of detentions, harassment and violent intimidation. The resistance has proven amazingly resilient. Repression has only added members to the trade union movement, which is now openly political in its objectives. International business has begun to get the message that until South Africa becomes a stable, democratic, non-racial state, further investment will be unprofitable and foolish.

It is a testimony to the discipline, commitment and reasonableness of the forces of resistance that South Africa has arrived at this state of affairs. A low-scale civil war continues. Ultimately, the rule of the majority is inevitable. For citizens of Canada and the United States, the question becomes how we can best help the inevitable to happen—sooner, less violently and with greater benefit to all.

Chapter Seven:

Kragdadigheit: A Total Strategy Against a Total Onslaught

The ultimate aim of the Soviet Union and its allies is to overthrow the present body politic in the Republic of South Africa and to replace it with a Marxist-oriented form of government to further the objectives of the USSR. Therefore all possible methods and means are used ... instigating social and labour unrest, civilian resistance, terrorist attacks against the infrastructure of South Africa, and the intimidation of black leaders and members of the security forces. This on-slaught is supported by a worldwide propaganda campaign and the involvement of various front organizations such as trade unions and even church organizations and leaders. [From a South African Government White Paper on Defence and Armaments Supply, 1982][1]

Since 1948 South African administrations have portrayed themselves as the heroes in a war between godless communism and Christian Western values. To be sure, there is never total agreement as to who is in which camp. On occasion, for instance, President Kenneth Kaunda of Zambia is portrayed as a black moderate, a man of peace. Yet the White Paper cited above calls his country "a Marxist satellite." South African radio sometimes portrays Botswana and Lesotho as "friendly to the Soviet Union," simply because African National Congress exiles have sometimes found shelter there. According to some South African media, the Soviet KGB is the real force behind the worldwide campaign to isolate South Africa through disinvestment and sanctions. Blacks, they claim, are being stirred up by outside exploitation of their grievances, which they would otherwise not be capable of feeling or protesting.[2]

By using this form of ideological simplification, the South African government tries to avoid the central dilemmas of white supremacy. By portraying all who oppose apartheid as communist-inspired, it not only deludes itself, creating a fear-dominated paranoia, but also tries to persude others who oppose communism to its view of the situation.

The latest phase of what the South African government sees as a war of two worlds began in 1977 when P.W. Botha became Prime Minister. Botha was a modern Afrikaner, determined to be sophisticated, efficient and rational. As Minister of Defense since 1966, he had become thoroughly familiar with the new breed of South African military leadership, some of whom emphasized that marginal political changes must accompany a military hard line. The new government decided it must have a "total strategy" against a "total onslaught."

A total strategy

The total strategy meant being prepared to use whatever force might be necessary to impose domestic order. At the same time, South Africa's economic domination of the region would impose a Pax Pretoria on all of southern Africa. South African military strategists believed that while urban opposition to the government could be crushed or controlled by military tactics, South Africa could not afford to fight both an internal and an external war at the same time. By making some marginal concessions in the apartheid system, the strategists believed they could weaken the internal appeal of revolutionary movements, yet preserve the essentials of white supremacy, relying on the use of force whenever necessary. Their approach to imposing regional peace has been to promote civil wars in nearby African nations which they see as friendly to liberation movements and to use economic leverage to establish control of the region. They also hoped to strengthen some groups of blacks identified by ethnic labels in South Africa who would be allies of the government. In these ways, they hope to save their own troops from direct military involvement as much as possible, while advancing modernized apartheid throughout southern Africa.

To carry out this strategy, a State Security Council (SSC) was created to coordinate and manage all aspects of national security. The SSC compares itself in function to the U.S. National Security Council, but it sees itself as more effective and efficient. As the focal point of national decision-making, the SSC makes policy and sees that it gets executed. The SSC serves as the primary cabinet committee on defense, foreign policy, many economic questions and some issues of constitutional reform and justice. Half of the

SSC staff are intelligence service personnel, and military officers are prominent in all high-level inter-departmental committees. The head of the intelligence service is secretary to the SSC, and the defense minister, General Magnus Malan, is a key adviser to Botha on all strategic and domestic issues.[3]

Cosmetic changes at the margins

South African propaganda makes much of recent reforms, claiming that apartheid is ended—but the reality is quite different.

The only reform that has significantly changed apartheid was the revision of the labor laws, which was result of the Wiehahn Commission's report (see Chapter Six). Other reforms, such as changes in the pass laws and in influx control laws and the proposed establishment of a common citizenship, have been either abandoned or executed in such a way as to strengthen apartheid. In no case have these "reforms" changed either the location of power under apartheid or its basic system.

Another political change promoted by "the total strategy" was cooptation of the "Coloured" and "Indian" population. By incorporating these "middle groups," apartheid planners hoped to buy them off with crumbs from the cake of power. In 1983, a new Constitution set up three parliaments: one for whites, one for "Coloureds" and one for "Indians," with the number of seats allocated according to the size of each population (a 4:2:1 ratio).* Seats in the white parliament thus total more than the combined seats of the others.

"Coloured" and "Indian" representatives can vote in their parliaments on their "own affairs." But on important common issues like defense spending and economic policy, the power of decision remains in white hands. To illustrate: in 1986 the "Indian" and "Coloured" chambers refused to agree to two national security laws making "emergency" powers "normal." The bills were then referred to the President's Council, which is dominated by Botha's white Nationalist party, and approved. Even such approval was not necessary; Botha could have simply declared them to be law.[4]

Imposing domestic order

As we saw in Chapter Six, opposition to the 1983 constitution led to massive and unprecedented mobilization of resistance forces.

---

* if blacks are counted as real people, the ratios shift significantly, to 26:6:3:1.

The government's response was equally unprecedented brutality. It used every legal and extra-legal means at its command to crush what it saw as a revolutionary upsurge by a militant but insignificant minority.

But the "insignificant" resisters have continued to require attention. From October 1984 on, South African troops have joined the police in creating a permanent army of occupation in all African townships. Police and army personnel have invaded classrooms and even become teachers. They have attacked funeral processions and church services. In many townships, black mercenaries hired by the government, like the *witdoeke* described in Chapter Four, have threatened, beaten up or assassinated local leaders.

When massive anti-apartheid demonstrations were impending on June 12, 1986, the eve of the tenth anniversary of the Soweto uprising, the government announced that it would declare a State of Emergency. In a classic explanation of *kragdadigheit* (toughness), P.W. Botha declared, "The world must take note and never forget that we are not a nation of 'weaklings.' "[5]

The State of Emergency was a confession that the "reform" phase of the national strategy was over. The reforms were thus exposed as merely shams. The continuing political turmoil was making business restless. As it had after Sharpeville, the government cracked down. It was determined to rule by force in the townships and to impose order—even if that meant sweeping away all of the activists it could find. By May 1987 at least 50,000 people had been either detained or forced into hiding. UDF and COSATU leaders led the arrest lists. The Detainees' Parents Support Committee estimated that of the 25,000 put in detention, 10,000 were children under 18, 3,500 were women and 12,500 were men.

The government also detained an unprecedented number of clergy, who were often subjected to torture. These included such prominent church leaders as Smangaliso Mkatshwa, secretary general of the Catholic Bishops' Conference; Sigisbert Mfaniseni Ndwandwe, Anglican Suffragan Bishop of Johannesburg; and Simon Farisani, a dean of the Evangelical Lutheran Church. Frank Chikane, described in Chapter One, was forced into hiding on the eve of his installation as the new secretary general of the South African Council of Churches in June 1987. The number of laypeople detained is in the thousands.

Another objective of the State of Emergency was tight control of the media. The government was especially anxious to stop television and radio reports of the brutal violence that the army and police were using against civilians. It also wanted to stop reports on the strength of the resistance. So journalists could no longer film, tape-record or photograph any clashes of the resistance with troops or police. They could no longer publish "subversive statements," meaning any criticism of the government, except as reports of court proceedings or Parliamentary debate. Newspapers appeared with blacked-out words or even huge blank spaces where the censor had deleted "subversive" material.

The militarization of the state

To measure the extent to which South Africa has become militarized, compare these military budget estimates from the last three decades:

1960/61:	44 million Rands
1975/76:	948 million Rands
1985/86:	4,274 million Rands

These figures may well be underestimates. One expert on military matters estimates that 20 percent of South African national expenditures goes into military spending.[6]

Over the same period, the size of the military has similarly mushroomed. In 1965 the military numbered only 26,500. But by 1985 there were 106,400 people in the regular army, navy, air forces and medical corps, with another 317,000 in the reserves, plus a further 21,000 listed as the South West Africa Territory Force.[7]

The number of whites available for military service is limited by the size of the white population (four to five million). Until fairly recently, national policy was to use blacks, "Coloureds" and "Indians" only in military duties that did not require the use of firearms. That philosophy has changed as the military's personnel needs increased. In 1963 the South Africa Defense Force (SADF) started the "Coloured" Corps. By 1983, 10,000 members of the Defense Force were not whites. Today, blacks are active in the Southwest Africa Territorial Force (SWATF)—the so-called "native forces" of Namibia—and in various "homeland" military units. But black units are not commanded by black officers.

A leading expert on the South African military, Kenneth Grundy, has pointed to the burden that war places on black shoulders:

> One can see that blacks bear a disproportionate burden of combat (compared to their numbers in the SADF itself). . . . Blacks can be regarded as 'cannon fodder.'. . . There is an

"economic draft" of sorts, forcing young blacks out of the private economy that holds little promise into a *relatively* well-paid and secure "job" in the SADF.[8]

Area Defense

While South African military thinkers claim that the African National Congress operates without much popular support, they also believe that the ANC's isolated bombing attacks "create an atmosphere of instability."[9]

Fear that the ANC would train guerillas in neighboring nations and then infiltrate them back across South Africa's borders led to the Defence Act of 1982, under which the government can call up auxiliary troops in selected areas that are under attack or are being infiltrated. In rural areas of the Transvaal, SADF has used white farming families' knowledge of the local terrain and local people to create an auxiliary defense force. Yet 40 percent of the farms along the border from Mozambique to Botswana no longer have any resident white farm families. Most of those who remain are heavily armed and live behind security fences; almost all of them believe that the guerillas will continue to increase their activities. Because of this threat, some areas of northern Transvaal and Natal are now under direct military rule.[10]

Under the National Key Points Act of 1980, the Minister of Defense can designate any premises a "National Key Point." The owners are then required to store weapons and communications equipment and to organize and train a defense unit to secure the Key Point against "terroristic" activities, sabotage, espionage or subversion. In the light of this law, international corporations with operations in South Africa cannot claim truthfully that their factories do or will have no military or political significance.[11]

Destabilizing the region

The "total strategy" is not aimed only at internal dissent. South Africa intends to dominate the entire region by keeping neighboring nations vulnerable and dependent.

South Africa is trying to preserve and extend the South African hegemony created by European colonial powers and by international corporations in the nineteenth and twentieth centuries. ("Hegemony" means dominant influence; we refer here to the strategy of deliberate linking of regional economies into a political and economic structure with its control center in South Africa.)

Acutely aware of this legacy, the nine other nations of the region, which are all independent and black-ruled, are determined to become less vulnerable to South Africa military and economic blackmail and penetration. By breaking these links, they want to create a balanced economy in which the black nations can help one another develop and prosper. This is a major reason why they formed the Southern African Development Coordination Conference (SADCC) in 1979.[12]

The formation of SADCC spurred South Africa's strategists to new levels of aggressive activity. The goals of their strategy to "destabilize" South Africa's neighbors and thus keep them under control appear to be:

1. To force neighboring nations to deny any facilities to the ANC or to SWAPO (the liberation movement of Namibia): no transit rights, training sites, bases, offices, political presence and, ideally, no ANC or SWAPO members in exile.

2. To prevent neighboring states from supporting mandatory sanctions against South Africa.

3. To deny to the Soviet Union or its allies any political or military role in the region.

4. To eliminate all forms of government that seem (even rhetorically) to be in favor of socialism.

5. To maintain and strengthen the neighboring countries' economic links with and dependence on South Africa.

6. To incorporate the nations in the region into a "constellation of states" whose controlling center would be South Africa.[13]

In attempting to achieve these goals, South Africa's heavily militarist administration pursues a variety of military, economic and diplomatic tactics, which we will now outline.

The military occupation of Namibia

The most flagrant example of direct military aggression by South Africa against its black neighbors is its occupation of Namibia, the mineral-rich desert country that adjoins its northwest frontier.

South Africa invaded Namibia in 1915, during World War I. Namibia was then a German colony called Southwest Africa. After the war, the League of Nations gave South Africa the right to rule that land as trustee for the Namibian people. The Namibian people's rights to determine their future and their form of gov-

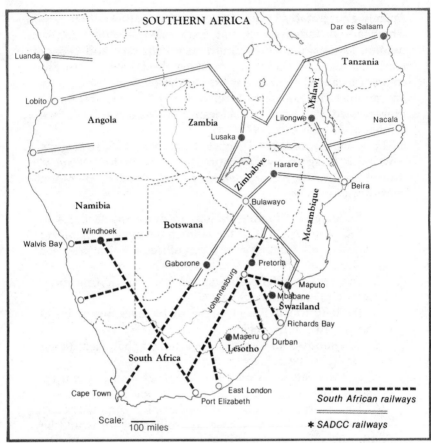

SOUTHERN AFRICA

Luanda
Lobito
Angola
Namibia
Windhoek
Walvis Bay
Botswana
Gaborone
South Africa
Cape Town
Port Elizabeth
East London
Durban
Lesotho
Maseru
Richards Bay
Swaziland
Mbabane
Maputo
Pretoria
Johannesburg
Zimbabwe
Bulawayo
Harare
Zambia
Lusaka
Lilongwe
Malawi
Mozambique
Beira
Nacala
Tanzania
Dar es Salaam

Scale: ⎯⎯⎯⎯
        100 miles

━ ━ ━ ━ ━ South African railways

═══════ SADCC railways

* The countries that belong to the Southern African Development Coordination Conference (SADCC) are: Angola, Botswana, Mozambique, Tanzania, Zambia, Zimbabwe, Lesotho, Malawi and Swaziland.

ernment were recognized, but South Africa was to serve as a "tutor" in how to be "civilized." But South Africa ruled Namibia for its own economic benefit, turning it, in effect, into a province of its own. It ignored the rights of the people and treated them as ignorant and inferior, fit only to serve the interests of whites, who are only 5 percent of the population of Namibia.

Because of South Africa's human rights abuses in Namibia and because it had not honored its mandate to prepare the Namibian people for independence, the United Nations (in 1966) and the International Court of Justice (in 1971) declared that South Africa's right to occupy and rule the country had ended. South Africa must withdraw and let the U.N. administer the territory until the

Namibian people had a chance to decide their own destiny.

The U.N. Security Council repeatedly set deadlines for withdrawal, but South Africa ignored them, knowing that it could count on Britain, the United States and (until lately) France to veto punitive sanctions. Instead, it promoted long constitutional talks with various hand-picked political groups. But these talks, leading to carefully crafted "internal settlement," could not lead to an internationally acceptable solution.

In 1978, therefore, the U.N. set up a plan under Resolution 435 by which Namibia would become independent. It called for withdrawal of all combat troops, free and fair elections under U.N. supervision and a constitutional convention elected by universal franchise. At first South Africa seemed to accept the plan, but it soon became clear that it intended to stay in Namibia regardless of world opinion. It put forth excuse after excuse, the latest one being its fear of Cuban troops in Angola.

With U.S. support, South Africa has made the withdrawal of Cuban troops from Angola a condition of its withdrawal from Namibia. But South Africa's illegal occupation of Namibia long predates the 1975 arrival of Cubans in Angola, who came to help Angola repel a South African invasion.

South Africa's real reasons for staying on are economic and military. Namibia is rich in resources: minerals, abundant offshore oil and fishing grounds, cattle and sheep, and beautiful desert and wilderness areas. Even more important is Namibia's role as a buffer zone to keep African forces of liberation away from South Africa's borders. More than 100,000 South African Defense Force soldiers, police and paramilitary forces now occupy Namibia. A secret police unit called COIN (Counter-insurgency unit) or KOEVOET terrorizes the population, detaining and torturing thousands. South African forces have attacked churches, schools and hospitals. Northern Namibia, where half the population lives, is an "operational zone" with dusk-to-dawn curfews. The war, carried out at a cost of $1 million a day, is allegedly to prevent "terrorists" and the "tools of Moscow" from gaining control.

Namibians have long resisted foreign occupation. The Southwest African Peoples' Organization (SWAPO), started in 1960 to carry out nonviolent protest campaigns, turned to armed liberation tactics in 1966 because its nonviolence was met with brutality. Most observers believe that SWAPO would win any free and fair election in Namibia by a wide margin; even some South African officials concede the point. But instead of cooperating with the

U.N. plan to test popular leadership in an election, South Africa has installed a series of unpopular, ineffective governments who want Namibia "independent" under South African protection.

Aggression against independent neighbors

South Africa seems to be trying to turn back the pages of history; it has expended a great deal of military and strategic effort on neighboring countries that have become independent as a result of the liberation wars of the 1960s and '70s. Angola, Mozambique and Zimbabwe have borne most of the brunt of South Africa's military offensives and economic sabotage. With Botswana and the two small countries of Lesotho and Swaziland, these six nations and their relationships to South Africa are crucial to understanding of the strategy South Africa uses to maintain apartheid.

1. Angola

In 1974, after more than a decade of wars with African liberation movements, the Portuguese army overthrew Lisbon's fascist government and prepared to transfer power to the African movements of Angola, Mozambique and Guinea Bissau. In Angola there were three movements: The Popular Movement for the Liberation of Angola (MPLA), the National Front for the Liberation of Angola (FNLA) and the National Union for the Total Independence of Angola (UNITA). None were militarily strong; UNITA was the weakest. The three movements agreed to form a joint transitional government pending elections. But a civil war soon broke out in which the U.S. Central Intelligence Agency backed FNLA and UNITA against the MPLA. The U.S. Secretary of State, Henry Kissinger, decided in favor of covert U.S. intervention against the MPLA because the MPLA had had assistance and support from the Soviet Union and Cuba.

In October 1975, when it appeared that MPLA had gained the upper hand, South African troops launched an invasion of Angola with the support of FNLA and UNITA. MPLA then called on Cuba for emergency help. The airlifted Cuban troops succeeded in stalling the South Africans in their drive to take over the the Angolan capital. African countries rallied behind MPLA, and the U.S. Congress halted CIA intervention by passing the Clark Amendment. Claiming betrayal by the U. S., South Africa withdrew its troops from Angola. In a year's time, all nations except the United States and South Africa had recognized the MPLA government.

The UNITA movement has been built around the charisma of Jonas Savimbi. Some missionaries who served in Angola at the time believe Savimbi could have been elected the first president of Angola. But his willingness to enter into alliances with the Portuguese, the CIA and South Africa have gradually led to his ostracism by African countries except Zaire, which has allowed the CIA to use its territory for supplying UNITA and FNLA forces. After the debacle of 1975-76, Savimbi turned to South Africa for major support and received it.

In 1981, encouraged by the Reagan Administration's new policy of "constructive engagement" with South Africa, the South African Defense Force (SADF) began a new war in southern Angola. In its biggest operation, 5,000 South African troops advanced to Cahama, 80 miles north of the Namibian frontier. There they were stopped by the Angolan army, which was now significantly better trained than it had been when South African first invaded in 1975. Nevertheless, in 1981 towns were flattened; 130,000 Angolans became refugees and fled northward, further burdening the Angolan government. South African forces established a buffer zone of occupation in south central Angola from which to attack towns, military bases, and oil and power installations.

By 1984, 600,000 people had been displaced by South Africa's military actions or those of UNITA, which South Africa has helped to train and equip. Total damages to Angola caused by the war in the last ten years are estimated at $10 billion, more than all the foreign aid supplied to all the countries of southern Africa in the same period.

Notwithstanding the Lusaka Accord of 1984 (an agreement prompted by U.S. diplomats), South Africa's aggressive strategy toward Angola is still being carried forward with the help of its black ally, UNITA. After the 1985 repeal of the Clark Amendment, which had prohibited military aid to any Angolan group, the CIA resumed the supply of arms, equipment and training to UNITA.

In the course of the war, many oil, rail and power facilities have been destroyed. A 1987 UNICEF study found that in the previous year over 55,000 Angolan infants or children had died as a result of the war, and that in 1985 at least 10,000 civilians had been mutilated. Health workers, clinics, schools and vehicles carrying health and relief supplies are "deliberately chosen as targets of war for the purpose of causing a breakdown in civil administration and making large areas . . . ungovernable," according to the study. The Angolan government and international relief agencies such as the Red Cross say that UNITA regularly plants landmines in farm fields and footpaths, resulting in food shortages and over 20,000 amputees. UNITA denies that it planted mines to disrupt food production and claims that the government also plants mines. The results speak for themselves. Food production, which the government is trying to foster, has plummeted.[14]

South Africa often covers up its operations against Angola by claiming that they are the work of UNITA.[15] Clearly, UNITA is unable to win the war or even defend itself against the Angolan army without South African help. In September 1985, Defense Minister Magnus Malan admitted that South Africa had used army and air power to defend UNITA forces against being wiped out by Angolan troops. He appealed to the U. S. for help: "If these forces should wipe out Savimbi, then South Africa will be able to say that she did her bit to sustain this anti-Marxist force."[16]

The United States responded positively to this appeal. The Reagan Administration and the Congress not only repealed the Clark Amendment but funneled $15 million in so-called "covert aid" to UNITA. Since an embargo prevents arms shipments through South Africa, the United States now ships arms to UNITA through an air base in Zaire. The Organization of African Unity and the SADCC countries have condemned UNITA for acting as an agent of South African destabilization and for undermining regional development.[17]

2. Mozambique

Unlike Angola's, Mozambique's economy had long been intertwined with that of South Africa. Because Mozambique's southern province lies directly east of Johannesburg, the city of Maputo was developed as the principal port for minerals from South Africa's Transvaal mines. Historically, a huge part of Mozambique's revenues came from supplying rail links and port services to South Africa and Rhodesia. During Portuguese rule, more than 100,000 Mozambicans worked in the mines of South Africa, sending home wages that translated into valuable foreign exchange for Mozambique.

In 1977, after Mozambique had won its independence from Portugal, South Africa set out deliberately to sabotage the Mozambican economy, progressively its reducing rail traffic to a fraction of its earlier use and reducing the number of Mozambican migrant workers by more than half.[18] Up to 1985, the Mozambican economy lost an estimated $4 billion as well as the loss of 100,000 lives because of South African and Rhodesian aggression.

When it became an independent country in 1975, Mozambique had a per capita income of only $177 per year and almost no foreign exchange reserves. The next year Mozambique closed its border with Rhodesia to comply with U.N. sanctions, thus depriving itself of a third of its normal revenue from rail and port charges. Several years of war with Rhodesian guerrillas also took their economic toll.

In spite of these difficulties, Mozambique's economy seemed to be making progress in 1980 and 1981. Cashews, cotton, sugar and coal production were at their highest levels since independence. Zimbababwe, the new nation that replaced Rhodesia, was now headed by Robert Mugabe, who had developed close ties with Mozambique's Frelimo government. (Frelimo is a Portuguese acronymn for the liberation movement that in 1974 freed Mozambique from Portuguese rule.) The party that Mugabe headed had fought its war for independence in close collaboration with Frelimo. By 1983 Zimbabwe had re-routed 54 percent of its trade with the world through Mozambique and away from South Africa.[19]

In 1981, however, South Africa launched a military operation to destroy these gains. South African intelligence forces had recruited and trained a mercenary army. At its core was a group called the Mozambican National Resistance (MNR) or "Renamo," which had been founded in 1977 under the sponsorship of Rhodesian intelligence forces aided by former members of the Portuguese army and secret police.

The MNR destroyed vital railway lines from Zimbabwe to Maputo and was notorious for its brutality; its soldiers attacked civilians mercilessly, especially those traveling by rail and road. In the countryside, the MNR set out to create starvation, burning peasants' grain storage bins, destroying hundreds of rural shops, decimating whole villages with their medical centers and primary schools. The MNR recruited new members by kidnapping and by offering a higher standard of living to poor, illegal Mozambican migrants in South Africa and Swaziland.

The destabilization campaign was catastrophic for Mozambique. When combined with the worst drought in living memory, it produced economic collapse and starvation. Moreover, the Mozambican government had not yet won the support of many traditional farmers, who represent 10 million of Mozambique's 11 million people. In order to increase food production for the cities quickly, the government had concentrated on big agricultural development projects, but these proved to be larger than inexperienced Mozambican managers were able to handle. In addition, the war ruined cash crops that could be exported. With neither export nor port fee income, Mozambique had no foreign exchange with which to import commodities. There was nothing for farmers to buy in the shops: no clothes, no knives, no kerosene lamps. So why should they produce? If Frelimo could not deliver the goods, why support them? In the end, many peasants came to a de facto truce with MNR, fearing reprisals if they did not.[20]

Overwhelmed by these difficulties and facing famine, the Mozambican government decided to court the Western capitalist powers. President Machel visited Europe to seek private investment. He asked the United States, Portugal and Britain to provide food aid and to press South Africa to stop its MNR support. By October 1983, when the West decided to give food aid, it was too late: 100,000 people had already starved to death.

On March 16, 1984, in the border town of Nkomati, Mozambique signed a public peace treaty with South Africa. Under the treaty, Mozambique was required to expel nearly all members of the African National Congress within its borders and to stop all transit through its territory by ANC soldiers. South Africa was to shut down its support of MNR. The United States acted as a broker in arranging this pact. Frelimo kept its part of the bargain, causing bitterness in the ANC. But the only part of the bargain that South Africa kept was to shut down an MNR radio station.

> Far from bringing peace, [the] Nkomati [treaty] brought an escalation in the war. . . . Just prior to the Accord . . . there was a massive resupply effort in order to keep the MNR going as long as possible. . . .
>
> Soon after the signing . . . Malawi* expelled the MNR representative there . . . yet the use of Malawi as a rear base increased. . . . Throughout 1985 the MNR was able to use Malawi to launch invasions.[21]

In September 1985 the Mozambique government produced captured documents which clearly demonstrated that the South African military had no intention of following the arrangements

---

* Malawi is a country situated like a sword aimed at the Mozambique coastline. With South African backing, MNR has used its Malawi base to deepen this wedge and cut Mozambique in two.

of diplomats. In notes of a meeting between MNR and and South African military intelligence, General van der Westhuizen was reported to have told the military chief of MNR: "We, the military, will continue to give [the MNR] support without the consent of our politicians in a massive way so that [MNR] can win the war."[22]

The fact is that neither South Africa's military nor its senior politicians had ever had any intention of fully observing the terms of the Nkomati Accord.

In October 1986, Samora Machel, Mozambique's charismatic and dynamic president and several high-ranking Mozambican officials were killed when the plane in which they were flying home crashed in South African territory. In spite of an official South African assessment blaming pilot error, many people in Mozambique and elsewhere believed it likely that a navigational beacon in South Africa lured the pilot off course as he tried to find Maputo airport.[23]

Meanwhile, the MNR continues its attacks. A Mennonite volunteer who was in Homoine, a small town in Mozambique's southern province, on July 18, 1987, when MNR slaughtered 380 of the town's residents, summed up his feelings:

> This is not a civil war. These people are not fighting for any ideal. They're fighting to create terror.
>
> In Homoine poeple now are walking the streets with glassy eyes. They don't know what to do. Go back to work? The only reason they are there is because rice, food and clothes are being given away. . . . A lot came to Homoine because they thought it was secure. . . . In the villages the people I work with sleep in the corn fields because they cannot stay in their houses at night. . . . It's a war of terror and it's not going to stop until the people who are supporting it, which is South Africa, are stopped.[24]

3. Zimbabwe

The overwhelming election victory of Robert Mugabe's party, the Zimbabwe African National Union (ZANU), in 1980 shocked South Africa. For years South Africa had helped Rhodesia in its war to maintain white supremacy by supplying troops, equipment and sanctions-breaking supplies of vital equipment and oil. Now, after eight years of a war for liberation, Rhodesia had been replaced by Zimbabwe, a country ruled by the black African majority. South Africa had anticipated that Bishop Abel Muzorewa, whom it had favored, would be the new prime minister. Although 30,000 ZANU guerilla fighters had taken over the countryside with the help of the local population, South Africa had continued to believe that ZANU had little popular support.

In the wake of Zimbabwe's 1980 election, South Africa attempted to strangle the new nation in its cradle with bombings, assassination attempts and military sabotage. South Africa continues to sponsor dissidents in Zimbabwe and to train them in the northern Transvaal, assisted by former Rhodesian intelligence officers. But the most harmful way South African works to destabilize Zimbabwe is by economic sabotage.

During the war for liberation of Rhodesia, South Africa became Rhodesia's most important trade partner. After Mozambique closed its frontier to Rhodesian traffic in 1976, all of Rhodesia's exports and imports went through South Africa. After Zimbabwean independence, South Africa was determined to demonstrate that a black-run African state would end in economic disaster. In January 1981 South Africa imposed an informal embargo on goods bound for Zimbabwe. In March 1981, when Zimbabwe voted in favor of sanctions against South Africa at the United Nations, the South African government retaliated by ending its bilateral trade agreement with Zimbabwe. In April, South African Railways demanded the return of twenty-four locomotives leased to Zimbabwe. South Africa then delayed fuel bound for Zimbabwe, which was forced to start rationing gasoline. Migrant mineworkers from Zimbabwe were expelled from South Africa, which meant that much-needed earnings were lost. Zimbabwe's oil supply was jeopardized when the MNR, aided by South African agents, attacked the oil pipeline and the railway to Beira, the port city of central Mozambique. In 1982, South African commandos blew up the Beira oil storage depot.

In the end South Africa's attempt was unsuccessful. Zimbabwe was able to buy new locomotives and to shift cargo to Mozambique. In many areas of public life the government began to weed out the "Rhodies," whites committed to maintaining the old regime and to undermining the new. Zimbabwe has continued to favor sanctions against South Africa.

South Africa's most pressing reason for putting the squeeze on Zimbabwe is Zimbabwe's central position in the Southern African Development Coordination Conference (SADCC). The key to SADCC's plans to sever the dependence of most of its nine members on South Africa is the restructure of the region's transport system. Zimbabwe is the key country for transport because it handles traffic from Zambia and Botswana and it exports more than any country in the region except South Africa. By using Mozambique's three main ports (plus Dar es Salaam in Tanzania), Zimbabwe and the other SADCC member states hope to provide an alternative to shipping through South Africa. To provide one alternative route, the Zimbabwe government and the SADCC have now created a Beira Corridor corporation with the help of private corporations. And thousands of Zimbabwean and Tanzanian troops are defending Mozambique's transportation system.

Three hostage states

Three countries in the SADCC system are so dependent on South Africa that prying them loose is very difficult if not impossible. Botswana, Lesotho and Swaziland are former British High Commission territories that South Africa has always wanted to incorporate as parts of its bantustan confederation. While these three have resisted political incorporation, they are members of the South African Customs Union and function as part of the South African economy.

4. Swaziland: The Swazi royal family has benefitted from close relations with foreign corporations which have headquarters in South Africa. Most large Swaziland businesses are joint ventures; the king and his relatives enjoy shares along with foreign investors. The nation as such does not draw any returns from these investments. Swazi police have often collaborated with South Africa in tracking down and arresting liberation movement guerillas and political activists.

5. Lesotho: One of only two nations in the world that is entirely surrounded by another country, Lesotho is the perfect example of a hostage nation. There is no conceivable way that Lesotho can feed or provide employment for its people without South Africa. Some 150,000 Basotho (citizens of Lesotho), about 11 percent of the population, work in South Africa. Their earnings, plus revenues from the South African Customs Union, provide Lesotho with critical income. By threatening this income and by direct and indirect military intervention, South Africa has forced Lesotho to deport refugees related South African liberation movements. As it does in other neighboring countries, South Africa used African divisions and tensions to build up a dissident force. It equipped and trained the so-called Lesotho Liberation Army to oppose the government of Chief Jonathan Leabua. Leabua enjoyed South African support until he denounced apartheid and sheltered South African exiles, some of them with ANC connections.

In December 1982, South Africa gave Lesotho a taste of *kragda-digheit* in a display of brazen military intervention. In the dead of night, South African commandos stormed into Maseru, the capital city, killing forty-two people in their homes. Twelve of the dead were citizens of Lesotho; thirty were African National Congress members living in exile. None had any connection with ANC military activities. Then in May, June and July, South Africa kept food supplies from entering Lesotho and subjected Lesotho citizens to long delays at South African border posts. In September 1983 Lesotho was forced to expel twenty-four ANC-related exiles to comply with South African demands.

These concessions, however, only whetted South Africa's appetite for power. In January 1986, South Africa fomented and engineered a coup in which the Lesotho military deposed Leabua. Following the coup, Lesotho deported a large number of ANC-related refugees.

6. Botswana: While Botswana depends heavily on South Africa for food and for employment in mining and textile enterprises, which are based on South African capital, it has tried to safeguard the rights of refugees from South Africa, provided they do not use Botswana territory for armed incursions into South Africa or Namibia. Of course, Botswana's tiny 3,000-soldier army cannot completely control its long borders nor defend against incursions by South Africa's military.

Nonetheless, South Africa is determined to make Botswana sign an agreement like its Nkomati Accord with Mozambique. It deplores the mere presence in Botswana of persons with an ANC point of view. In June 1985 South African commandos invaded Gabarone, Botswana's capital, blew up ten houses, and killed fourteen persons, claiming that the houses were ANC bases. But only five of those killed had any connection with ANC and none of these had any known role in military actions.

Despite these attacks, Botswana has refused to be intimidated. At a recent SADCC meeting held in Botswana, the secretary general of ANC, Alfred Nzo, was an honored guest despite threats from Pretoria. But residents of Gabarone are now afraid to talk about South African politics at all.[25]

The smiling face of aggression

Kragdadigheit, the determined use of whatever force is necessary to crush all opposition and to retain white rule, is masked by righteousness. Numerous ways of voicing concern cloak this particular devil in saint's clothing.

One such cloaked concern comes in the cry, "We are up against communism." South African propagandists and many sincere Christian people in South Africa (as well as in the United States and Canada), believe that the issue of apartheid does not have to do with race or class so much as with Soviet "expansionism." At stake, it is alleged, is a Christian civilization under attack from a consummately evil Soviet Empire. Defining the issue in these terms gives South Africa several advantages. First, the issue of institutional racism and exploitation in one relatively small country shrinks to insignificance against the pageant of the struggle for global domination. Second, any criticism of apartheid is laid at the door of communists. And third, even while South Africa condemns all opposition from the outside world, it commands the support of Western nations in its battle with communism—strangely, the same Western nations who declare that they oppose apartheid.

As the struggle over apartheid gains momentum, South African apologists are prone to say, "Christian values are at stake." But as we have seen, the church in South Africa is harshly divided. Although the majority of South African Christians are black, the church as an institution has historically been in white hands. Today, black Christians have gained positions of official leadership and influence in many churches and have begun in many cases to organize active and effective opposition to apartheid. These leaders, joined by a minority of prophetic white Christians like Beyers Naudé, now say that the real issue is: Whose side is the church on? Does it side with white supremacy or with the black majority? Like Nazi Germany, however, the so-called Christian nation of South Africa has allies within the churches, both Dutch Reformed and English-speaking. And the *Kairos Document* of 1985, which we will examine in our next chapter, is compared by many to the Barmen Declaration, through which many Christians in Germany affirmed their loyalty to the one who reigns over all spheres of life—Jesus Christ—as opposed to "German" Christianity.

Arguing from negative examples

Supporters of continued white rule in South Africa often point to black Africa as an illustration of the consequences of majority rule: mismanaged economies, "tribal" wars and undemocratic, one-party systems. "Black Africa is a mess; it needs South Africa to survive," some say. South Africa in fact does have resources that could help develop the region, but none of its neighbors wants to be wholly or even heavily dependent on another nation—regardless of whether it is ruled by whites or blacks. The nations of southern Africa understandably want to gain control over their own economies, especially over vital commodities like food.

Blaming African nations alone for their own underdevelopment ignores the direct legacy of European colonialism, which created the unbalanced and underdeveloped economies. Black nations inherited enormous difficulties. Lack of basic education and health care as well as of service management skills, to name only a few, are serious obstacles to development. When Mozambique and Angola won their independence, for example, less than 10 percent of their people could read or write. Zimbabwe's literacy rate was higher, but even highly educated blacks had almost no experience in business or government management. The economic situation of the region was created by Western colonialism to serve its own needs; it was never intended to form the basis for strong, interdependent African economies.

Another rationale for continuing white rule is that "tribal warfare makes it necessary." And, to be sure, a number of African nations have experienced ethnic conflict. But again, most African nations were arbitrary creations of European colonial powers; original ethnic and political groups and boundaries were not taken into account. No one wants to go back to "tribal" rule, but loyalties to ethnic groups do make for difficulties in emerging black nations. A number of African nations, such as Tanzania and Zambia, have been able to overcome these divisions. Zimbabwe also is making progress in overcoming the split between ZAPU and ZANU, political parties that represent two different languages and traditions. South Africa, on the other hand, has deliberately sharpened ethnic divisions by reinforcing such ethnically based political parties as UNITA and the MNR. Its own "homelands" system deliberately contrives to divide Africans against their will by alleged "tribal" identity.

The one-party put-down

African nations are often portrayed as undemocratic because they are one-party states.

But a one-party system is not necessarily undemocratic. Most nations in the region have party congresses and conventions to which delegates are freely elected to ensure that the party is based in grass-roots thinking. To ensure national unity and to mobilize a concerted national plan for development, a single party is important to most African nations. The political loyalties and the military organizations of most African countries are newer and more fragile than those of Western countries; thus, a dissident group can easily mount a successful coup. Furthermore, when there are several political parties, they often tend to form along ethnic and regional lines (as some do in the United States and Canada), factionalism that young countries often cannot cope with.

When plying the one-party argument, South Africa makes much of the Idi Amin example. And clearly, Uganda is a beautiful land tragically wracked by civil war and violence that has cost hundreds of thousands of lives. But to picture all African leaders as potential Amins is a racist assumption. What about Zambia's Kenneth Kaunda, a deeply Christian thinker? Or Julius Nyerere of Tanzania, a Roman Catholic by upbringing and a person of great simplicity, humility and strength? Or Mozambique's beloved Samora Machel?

A rationale for failure

"If majority rule comes to South Africa, it will be an economic disaster," is another claim by proponents of white rule. Obviously, no one can predict the future exactly. But in looking at the present situation, there is little doubt that South African destabilization efforts have been the major cause of economic failure in Mozambique and Angola. SADCC has estimated that by 1984 destabilization had cost the nations of the region $10 billion (U.S.), an amount which equals a third of their total annual exports and surpasses all the foreign aid they have received. Current estimates of damage from 1984 to 1986 run to an additional $5 billion.

Some African nations have indeed mismanaged their economies. Tanzania and other countries are often cited as examples of bureaucratic bungling. But in many cases a nation's development priorities have actually been created by international lending agencies. Although the World Bank and the International Monetary Fund are now prescribing free market solutions for Africa's development, they have not always done so.

In the past, United States leaders fostered policies that stressed government direction of development in third-world countries in part because these leaders believed that free enterprise alone could not raise the living standards of the poor. Most third-world countries face a problem in dealing with the world market system, managed as it is by the developed world.

When the prices of export crops and minerals drop, as they often do when recession or technological change occurs in the industrialized world, third-world countries usually find that they can no longer pay for the imports of machinery, spare parts, fuel, fertilizers and food needed to keep their industries and farms producing. As their economies decline, so do their tax revenues. The governments are then forced to borrow to maintain the education, health care and other social service systems that people have expected since the end of colonialism. Fixed ceilings for food prices in cities, which amount to a subsidy to urban residents, appear to discourage farmers from producing. When the governments turn to the International Monetary Fund for help with the mounting crisis, they meet with demands for austerity that are bound to cause popular distress: cut government spending on health, education and social services; eliminate food subsidies and controlled prices; and devalue the currency. Adopting these measures results in a drastic cut in the real income of most people, and can lead to disastrous political ramifications.

Planning the future

The liberation movements of South Africa and Namibia are keenly aware of such political and economic difficulties. The Namibia Institute in Lusaka, Zambia, is already developing detailed plans for various sectors of a free Namibia. ANC plans in progress also take into account the economic experience of other African countries as well as building a political vision of a democratic, non-racist society. The ANC has taken pains to meet with South African business leaders and dissident white politicians to reassure them that, when the new society comes, it will not drive whites into the sea. On the contrary, white expertise and skill will be needed. But the ANC insists that the new democratic order must be reflected in a new economy:

> The democratic state will be representative of all the people
> of our country, and especially the ordinary working people

who own neither land nor factories and neither the mines nor the banks. It will therefore be called upon to ensure that the wealth of the country increases significantly and continuously and that it is shared equitably by all the people. . . . The new democratic order will necessarily have to address the question of ownership, control and direction of the economy as a whole to ensure that neither the public nor the private sectors serve as a means of enriching the few at the expense of the majority.[26]

The ANC has promised that the revolution, when it comes, will guarantee freedoms of speech, assembly, language, religion, the press—as well as freedom from arbitrary arrest and detention without trial. It has reassured those who fear a one-party dictatorship that people may form and join any party they wish.

These pledges hardly seem to constitute a threat of economic chaos. Rather, they seem the "assurance of things hoped for" which Hebrews 11 describes as *faith*. With seventy-five years of experience, the ANC is a seasoned movement with an impressive administrative, political and diplomatic record. Within South Africa are many black workers who have long experience in industry and mining, although not in corporation management. The trade union movement has also developed strong leaders. It is preposterous to presume that it is better to keep imposing apartheid by force than to allow blacks to lead South Africa and the region toward democratic, non-racist rule. Eliminating the economic costs of the military build-up that apartheid has forced on the region would bring an enormous economic blessing.

How strategic *is* South Africa?

A final argument in favor of continued white rule in South Africa is that "the strategic interests of the West are at stake." To bolster this point, much is made of the importance of the Cape of Good Hope to the military and naval forces of NATO. The Cape is indeed a strategic location: every year some 25,000 vessels pass it with such cargo as oil from the Middle East and Asia. But is the Cape sea route therefore so crucial that the West must be allied with an apartheid government to keep this passage from falling into Soviet hands? In the event of a major war, the most strategic Soviet points for submarine warfare would be the North Sea and other exits from Europe, not the Cape of Good Hope.

"What about South Africa's strategic minerals?" Certainly South

Africa is a treasure trove of minerals, some of them strategic. A 1980 study by the U.S. Congress found that the United States is critically dependent on four imported minerals: chromium, manganese, platinum and cobalt. Cobalt comes from Zaire and Zambia. South Africa and the Soviet Union are major suppliers of the other three, but there are alternative sources: chromium and platinum are available from Zimbabwe; Zambia has a fairly large proven manganese source, as does Angola. Since the U.S. and other importers have preferred to deal with South Africa, however, production from other African nations has been low. Assuming that a liberation movement came to power in South Africa, the new government would be likely to continue to sell minerals to the West because that is where the market is. After all, Angola, which has the backing of the Soviet Union, has very cordial relations with multi-national corporations operating its petroleum fields. In fact, most of Angola's trade is with the U.S.[27]

Summing it up

Militarization is the logical extension of a basic perception by the South African government that what matters in the end is power, not legitimacy or authority. Because racial domination has no moral or theological justification, it cannot be maintained except by the use of force, intimidation and lies.

Behind the South African militarists' talk about reforms and the abolition of apartheid looms their willingness to use whatever economic or military force may be necessary to maintain and even to extend white racist rule over all of southern Africa. In September 1986, President Botha made this position clear:

> The right to continued existence of each group, also the continued existence of the whites, must be maintained. It is not the case that we cannot deliver. It is the case that we will not deliver. Let there be no doubt about it. Nobody should ever expect us to confuse reform with surrender.[28]

A few days later the United States Congress enacted selective sanctions against South Africa. Inadequate though they were, they were a welcome signal that the West might have had enough of South Africa's *kragdadigheit*.

Chapter Eight:

The Liberation of Theology: On Which Side Shall the Church Be Counted?

> Amnesty International reported yesterday that another church in South Africa had been raided by security forces and some 70 worshippers taken into custody. . . . The raid took place on June 16. Reportedly, the people arrested had gone to pray for peace on the day on which many South Africans commemorate the deaths of black demonstrators in Soweto 10 years earlier. . . . Security troops in combat attire smashed the door and assaulted people in the church with rhinoceros-hide whips. [*The New York Times*, June 27, 1986]

A report such as this surely seems bizarre. Yet the event reported was not the only one of its kind: other churches were similarly raided and systematic detentions of clergy were under way. The offices of South African Council of Churches were invaded by police, who took stacks of its files and papers away.

Why should prayer have become so provocative, so dangerous? When the government announced a State of Emergency in 1986, it banned all commemorations of the June 16 Soweto uprising. But by what rationale could prayer be banned? A year earlier, a prophetic minority of laypeople and clergy had issued a "Call to Prayer" on June 16 for a "new and just order" in the land:

> We have continually prayed for the authorities, that they may govern wisely and justly. Now, in solidarity with those who suffer most, in this hour of crisis we pray that God in his grace may remove from his people the tyrannical structures of oppression and the present rulers in our country who persistently refuse to heed the cry for justice as reflected in the Word of God.[1]

These Christians called people to use the power of prayer, not the power of violence, but their call provoked a storm of opposition. South African conservative and liberal church leaders alike

denounced it. Most white Christian congregations disassociated
themselves from it. Anglican Archbishop Philip Russell agreed with
it theologically but saw that it would prevent future church
delegations from approaching the government to press for changes
in apartheid. Although the Call to Prayer deliberately avoided using
words like "the downfall of the government," or any other language
that might be interpreted as advocating violence, the press and
the government treated it as a call to revolution and to the violent
overthrow of the government.

The Call to Prayer challenged South African churches to translate
their repeated resolutions condemning apartheid into worship and
action. Were churches prepared to pray and work for the liberation
of South African *from* a tyrannical government or were they content
to pray *for* the tyrants? The Call to Prayer drew upon the theological
tradition of the Reformed Church represented by Calvin, Kuyper
and Barth, its greatest theologians, and on the natural law tradition
of the Roman Catholic Church. In both these traditions, to resist
tyranny and to struggle for liberty are indispensable obligations
of those who seek to obey God. Later, the grassroots leadership
of the churches amplified the Call's challenge in the *Kairos Document*,
which, as we will see, became even more controversial.[2]

In this chapter we shall examine some themes and issues posed
by these powerful challenges:

- Is there any theological or biblical justification for the
segregation of people by race, as the defenders of apartheid
argue?

- Is the racism of apartheid only a question of wrong attitudes
and beliefs, or is it also a question of economic and political
structures?

- How do we understand "violence"? Does violence happen
only when African township youths throw stones or ANC
"terrorists" attack police? Or can economic and political
structures be violent?

- If we agree that apartheid is a sin, what means may a
Christian use to fight against it? Is resistance to evil Christian?
Can a Christian ever embrace revolution, including the use
of force? Or is complete nonviolence the only acceptable
approach?

- How have the churches of South Africa, the United States

and Canada responded to the challenges set forth in the Call
to Prayer and the *Kairos Document?*

Is apartheid sin? Is it heresy to support it?

When we discuss whether apartheid is heretical, we treat it not
as a system of government but as an expression of theological
understanding. Is belief in segregating people by race justified
by a careful reading of the Bible?

The preponderant theological position in the white Dutch Reformed Churches of South Africa has been that God requires—
and therefore the church should work for—the separation of the
races. When the National Party came to power in 1948, the official
church newspaper said that "apartheid can rightfully be called
a church policy." To support this position, the theologians of
apartheid appealed to the Bible. In 1970, J. D. Vorster, Moderator
of the Dutch Reformed Church (NGK) in the Cape, defended
apartheid as biblical: "Our only guide is the Bible. Our policy and
outlook on life are based on the Bible. We firmly believe the way
we interpret it is right."[3] Was Vorster right?

The book of Genesis (1:1-2:4) describes the creation of a universe
intended to be in harmony and at peace. Adam and Eve are not
symbols of Hebrew experience alone; they stand for all humanity.
All human beings, Genesis tells us, are created in God's image.
We can be sure that being made in the image of God means that
each person is intended to live in a responsible relationship with
the Holy One, the Creator of all life. Each human being is precious
in God's sight. Each person is to have dominion over the world
(Genesis 1:28) as God's responsible representative, to be a co-
creator with God, and not to live as if he or she were utterly
self-defined. "Dominion" does not mean domination of others but
rather mutual interdependence in which each person's interests
are respected and honored. The dominion of human beings over
the rest of the creation means responsible stewardship over nature.

After the story of Creation, however, the Scriptures tell us about
the violation of God's intention: about sin. Separation, hostility
and disunity take over. Adam and Eve lose their innocence and
are driven from the garden. Cain kills his brother Abel. Sin reaches
its climax in the story of the Tower of Babel: human arrogance
results in a confusion of languages so extensive that nations can
neither understand one another nor comprehend one another's
cultures. The theological defenders of apartheid argue, however,

that this confusion of languages reasserts God's *original* intention to differentiate and separate people by races.

The sin illustrated by the Tower of Babel is pride, blind trust in technical prowess, brute force and national power, all of which the great empires and civilizations have typically exhibited. Each civilization's pride, growing from its anxiety to escape the responsibity of a relationship with God, brings forth the search to find security in corporate strength, power and fame:

> Come, let us build ourselves a city, and a tower with its top in the heavens, and let us make a name for ourselves, lest we be scattered abroad upon the face of the whole earth. [Genesis 11:4]

Redeeming human separateness

The rest of the Bible tells the story of God's mighty acts of redemption: God's work to restore the harmony and peace of the creation, which has been marred by sin. Isaiah prophesied that a time will come when the whole creation will be made new (Isaiah 11). All the great prophets challenged the rulers of Israel not to trust in military power or to rule over the people as did the pharaohs of Egypt but to rely on Yahweh's spirit (Isaiah 31). Zephaniah prophesied that in the process of redemption, God will reverse the Tower of Babel by granting "pure speech" (Zephaniah 3:9-11). And in the closing chapters of Isaiah, Yahweh proclaims: "I am coming to gather all nations and tongues" so that "they will come and see my glory" (Isaiah 66:18b; see verses 18-23).

Jesus Christ comes as the fulfillment of God's promises of reconciliation and peace:

> The Gospel . . . speaks of the infinite value of each individual person, the very hairs of whose head are numbered, and whom the Good Shepherd knows by name. It assures us that evil and death cannot have the last word. . . . [Jesus Christ] was sent into the world to effect atonement, at-one-ment; where there was disunity, division, alienation and estrangement, he established their opposites—fellowship, unity, togetherness, friendliness, community, peace and wholeness. [Desmond Tutu, in *Apartheid Is a Heresy*, p. 43]

The gift of the Holy Spirit at Pentecost, as recounted in the Acts of the Apostles, is the reversal of the Tower of Babel. In flames of fire, like a mighty wind, God's Spirit speaks through Jesus' disciples to people of all nations and tongues gathered in Jerusalem. The Spirit unites all who accept Christ into one Body and one People of God. This unity is shown in baptism, a sacrament that overcomes the barriers of language, culture and race yet, as the apostle Paul constantly emphasizes, affirms the diversity of spiritual gifts as well as differences in economic status, gender and culture. "For as many of you as were baptised into Christ have put on Christ. There is neither Jew nor Greek, slave nor free, male nor female, for you are all one in Christ Jesus" (Galatians 3:27-28).

Apartheid starts after the Fall

Apartheid theory starts from a very different theological premise from that contained in the Bible. It begins with the supremacy of sin and division. The rifts between peoples and cultures that have occurred throughout history become the rationale for making racial separation a theological imperative, a first principle:

> Apartheid turns [the New Testament] upside down. It claims that our different identities, our diversity, demand separation and disunity. That is to deny a central biblical truth. It is to say that Jesus Christ has not in fact broken down the middle wall of partition that used to separate the Jew from the Gentile, making of the two one people with a common access through the one Spirit to the Father. [Desmond Tutu, in *Apartheid Is a Heresy*, p. 43]

Apartheid begins with a pessimistic and cynical view of human nature akin to that of Thomas Hobbes, the seventeenth-century English political scientist who justified absolute monarchy on the ground that human beings are essentially greedy, violent, aggressive and competitive:

> True to its Hobbesian . . . orientation, white anthropology depicts a world in which every human self is the enemy of every other self. Not surprisingly, the government becomes the only power capable of preventing the "war of each against all and all against each.". . .White history books are full of stories about African fratricidal rivalries before [whites] came to secure peace between various ethnic groups. And as soon as the whites had settled, history becomes one in which the crude brutalities that either blacks or whites suffered at the hands of one another must necessarily predominate. . . . Nothing good or creative was to be found among blacks

because they were ... brutish beings with "no order in Nature, no shame, no truth." [Simon Maimela, in *Apartheid Is a Heresy*, pp. 51-52]

We saw in Chapter Three that, following the Sharpeville massacre of 1960, the international community of churches and the ecumenical movement in South Africa challenged apartheid as sinful doctrine. After Soweto in 1976, the Lutheran World Federation declared that apartheid is a system so perverted and oppressive that for the church it constitutes a *status confessionis*, literally, a situation that calls the church to confess (declare) its faith. Thus, on the basis of faith and to demonstrate Christian unity, all churches should publicly and unequivocally reject the apartheid system.[4]

Reformed Alliances declare apartheid to be heresy

The most important attack on the theology of apartheid came from within the Reformed Church itself. In 1981 the newly formed Alliance of Black* Reformed Christians in Southern Africa accused the Reformed tradition in South Africa of being "responsible for political oppression, economic exploitation, unbridled capitalism, social discrimination and total disregard for human dignity." Being Reformed, the Alliance charged, has come to be "equated with total, uncritical acceptance of the status quo, sinful silence in the face of human suffering, and manipulation of the Word of God in order to justify oppression." In the name of the true Reformed tradition, the Alliance declared that "apartheid is a sin and . . . the moral and the theological justification of it is a travesty of the Gospel, a betrayal of the Reformed tradition, and a heresy." So long as the white Dutch Reformed Churches accepted apartheid, justified it morally and theologically, and refused to declare it sin, there could no longer be any dialogue with them.

The United Congregational Church of South Africa, another church in the Reformed tradition, endorsed the Alliance's position and so did the South African Council of Churches. The Black Reformed Christians then appealed to the General Council of the World Alliance of Reformed Churches which was to meet in Ottawa in 1982.

---

* The Alliance defined "black" to mean "a condition and an attitude and not merely the pigmentation of one's skin." Some blacks have opted to be on the side of the oppressor and some whites have opted to be on the side of the oppressed.

Not only did the General Council of the Reformed Churches of the world affirm that apartheid is a sin and its moral and theological justification heresy, it suspended the Nederduitse Gereformeerde Kerk (NGK) and the Nederduitse Hervormde Kerk van Afrika (NHK) from the privileges of the World Alliance until:

1. Black Christians are no longer excluded from church services, especially the Holy Communion;
2. Concrete support in word and deed is given to those who suffer under the system of apartheid (or "separate development" as some defenders now call it);
3. The NGK and NHK synods make formal, unequivocal resolutions rejecting apartheid and committing themselves to dismantling apartheid in both church and politics.

In addition to suspending these two South African member churches, the World Alliance testified to its support for liberation from the "horrendous injustice, suffering and degradation of black Africans for whom Christ died," by electing Allan Boesak, a leading liberation theologian of the so-called "Coloured" mission of the NGK, to be its president.[6]

The Anglican Church of the Province of South Africa joined the World Alliance in pronouncing apartheid a denial of Christian faith because it teaches the irreconcilability of certain races. The Anglican Synod's 1982 resolution called apartheid "unChristian, evil and a heresy" and called on the white Dutch Reformed Church (NGK) to join in denouncing it as unscriptural. The Methodist Church similarly appealed to the Dutch Reformed Church to reject apartheid.[7]

The NHK, whose constitution excludes blacks from membership, withdrew from the World Alliance, attacking it because it "assails the authority of Holy Scripture" and "politicizes and socializes the person and work of Jesus Christ in a biased manner." The NGK, however, has moved toward acceptance of the fact that apartheid cannot be justified on biblical grounds while at the same time it retains segregated structures. White congregations retain local veto power over integration.[8]

While South Africa's English-speaking churches have for years rejected apartheid, the more important issue is whether they have acted to reverse their own racist and segregationist practice. In this respect, they have little to brag about, as church historian John deGruchy has noted:

The failure of the NGK and the NHK to recognize apartheid as a heresy does not give the so-called English-speaking Churches any cause for self-righteous satisfaction or judgment. Their complicity in racism in practice . . . is becoming ever more apparent as scholars begin to examine church history. . . . Confessing the faith against the heresy of apartheid has . . . the potential for a static confessionalism. . . . They too must be called to repentance and openness to the living word of the Gospel.[9]

Apartheid as a structure of violence

All societies use some form of coercion to maintain a certain structure—a set of laws, historical practices and an order of relationships. This social structure generally benefits some people more than others, creating "haves" and "have nots." The wider the gap in benefits between the haves and the have-nots, the greater the force that must be used to keep the have-nots in conformity with the social structure and its rules. City dwellers in the United States and Canada, for example, who earn good incomes and own nice houses tend to be supporters of law and order, efficient police, tough judges and strict application of the law. They do so in order to preserve their own property, income and economic status. Some segments of the population, often referred to as "the minorities," are likely to lack good education, opportunities for jobs and access to decent housing. From these have-not segments come a preponderance of those who commit crimes. We tend to see the robberies, muggings and rapes that they commit as a form of violence, but we tend *not* to see that lack of education, income, jobs or housing may also be a form of violence. The have-nots are breaking the rules of the system, but the system is also breaking them. Historic structures of discrimination create much of the misery of the poor who are black or Hispanic or women. Such structures often go unseen by the haves but are glaringly obvious to the have-nots. In the United States and Canada, the have-nots to some degree have been able to appeal to guarantees of certain fundamental rights, such as the Fourteenth Amendment of the U.S. Constitution.

In South Africa, the inequality between the haves and the have-nots is so huge that the enforced social structure, which exists to some degree in every society, becomes highly visible and highly violent. The haves are the white minority. The have-nots are the black majority. Those of the black majority have no fundamental rights protected by any constitution; whatever rights they may have had at one time have been taken away. Such a visible form of structural violence assaults our conscience. We can see that the majority of people are poor and denied power in a land that produces riches for, and grants power to, a minority.

Those who have seen a film or T.V. show about South Africa will probably have heard the cry, "Amandla ngwethu!" (Power! It shall be ours!) shouted at a rally in an African township by a crowd who brandish their fists to show that they are united and powerful in their solidarity. Why are slogans like these so important in South Africa? We all know what power feels like. For example, it feels good and fulfilling to have a skill and to be able to use it—to understand human anatomy or to produce crops successfully or to teach children so that they enjoy learning. It feels good to be able to shape a public policy and to make decisions. Having such powers helps us to enjoy the blessings of creation, to have responsible dominion as co-creators with God (Genesis 1:27-31). Since the creation is by its nature good, we must not assume that power in and of itself is evil. It is rather a gift of God, a trust to be used wisely and responsibly. To exercise that stewardship well requires that the good of all the people be taken into account (see Romans 13 and John 19:1).

When power is deliberately denied to one group and reserved for another group on an arbitrary basis like race, God's purpose of love is frustrated. The unity and reconciliation which God has effected in Christ is denied. Our possibilities become impossibilities. The potential to exercise our abilities, to accquire skills and to use our capacities to make decisions, to live fulfilling lives and even to exist physically is wasted and squandered.

The ultimate expression of powerlessness is to be slaves in perpetuity to masters who exploit people as tools, to be kept or discarded at will and to be kept ignorant, impotent and unskilled. As the Law and the Prophets again and again made clear, the people of Israel must never forget that they had once been slaves. Because Yahweh had liberated them, they must establish an equal society, not one based on exploitation. (See Leviticus 25; Deuteronomy 15; Amos 6). Whether in ancient Israel or contemporary South Africa, when the prosperity of the land is not shared, when the rich grind the faces of the poor to achieve wealth, the Exodus is forgotten, Yahweh's compassion and mercy for the poor and the oppressed is denied. When power is monopolized, those who are shut out live a kind of death. Their possibilities shrivel up and die like "raisins in the sun."

In South Africa this very day, some 136 African children will die of malnutrition; every day another 136 die (on average). They do not die because there is no food in the land. They do not die because there has been drought or because no one knows how to grow crops: South Africa is the seventh largest exporter of food in the world. The reason these children die is that their families—black families—are systematically denied access to land, income-producing jobs, knowledge, health care and the other "good things of life" that whites enjoy and take for granted. As we have seen in Chapter Four, apartheid starves blacks in other ways as well. Keeping blacks powerless and ignorant is not accidental. It is a deliberate policy. To subjugate so many people, force must be used by the minority: tyranny becomes a necessity.

Apartheid as a political tyranny

All governments make mistakes and commit acts of injustice from time to time. Tyranny, however, goes beyond such occasional actions. A tyranny by definition is a government established on a principle of benefit for only one group of people and not for the good of all.

Arguing from within the natural law tradition, South African theologian Albert Nolan, a Roman Catholic Dominican priest, argues that the apartheid government by its very nature is incapable of being reformed because it is in principle a tyranny:

> It is a minority government, elected by one small section of the population with the explicit mandate of governing the country for the benefit of, and in the interests of, the white community. . . . It is hostile to the common good, so it is not even in the best interests of the white minority. Nor could one hope or expect such a minority government to experience a change of heart and totally abandon the policy of apartheid. It has no mandate from its electorate to do so.
>
> . . . As members of the oppressed majority become more insistent and put more and more pressure on the tyrant . . . , the more tyrannical will this government become. . . . It will use . . . detentions, trials killings, torture, bannings, propaganda, states of emergency and other desperate and tyrannical methods. . . . Its reforms must ensure that the white minority remains on top.[10]

Arguing from within the Reformed tradition, Allan Boesak points out that John Calvin, the greatest theologian and reformer in that tradition, warned the King of France in the sixteenth century:

> For where the glory of God is not made the end of government, it is not a legitimate sovereignty but a usurpation. . . . Your first task as a ruler is to build your kingdom on justice . . . but if you allow yourself to be misled, you make of yourself a participant in injustice and your government will be nothing but gangsterism.[11]

Boesak argues that the South African government is "not a legitimate authority but a usurpation, not an agent of justice but, in the words of Augustine, a 'gang of robbers.'"[12] A careful interpretation of Romans 13 emphasizes the state's obligation to rule for "your good" as a servant of God for justice's sake, rather than the Christian's obligation to submit blindly to any state no matter how tyrannical it may become. As Boesak describes the situation:

> In its ongoing oppression and exploitation of the people, in its wanton violence in order to maintain the system, in its persistent disobedience of the word of God, [the South African] government can no longer claim to be the "servant of God for your good." It has become, quite simply, the beast from the sea [described in] Revelation 13, the biblical opposite of the servant of God of Romans 13.
>
> It is our responsibility—indeed, our duty—to resist this government. . . . [A Confessing Church that resists] overcomes evil in the way of Jesus Christ by challenging evil . . . by itself joining the oppressed in solidarity and unrestricted love; by facing evil with the willingness to give up one's life for the sake of others.[13]

On the other hand, President Botha and many church theologians in South Africa argue, in the phrases of Romans 13, that the state has been given the sword by God and that its subjects have no option but to obey. Botha has compared South Africa's war against "terrorists" and its attacks on neighboring nations like Botswana to Jesus' purifying the temple of moneylenders and traders. But for many black church people, Botha's statement is blasphemy, "the abomination of desolation," a desecration of the Holy, because he equates apartheid's military juggernaut with the church. Once more Caesar is claiming the right to be worshipped as God.[14]

The question of legitimate means of resistance

Some churchpeople argue that nonviolent means are in principle the only kind that Christians can employ to resist evil of any kind, even apartheid. Peace is not simply the *goal*, they say; peaceful *means* are the only way to achieve a lasting and just social order. Violence taken up even as a temporary expedient corrupts the spirit, destroying both the person and the movement and making the goal of a just society impossible.

Mohandas Gandhi is often taken as a model by those who believe that Christians should use only nonviolent means to bring about a just order in South Africa. Gandhi influenced Martin Luther King's belief that Christians must break the cycle of violence with nonviolence and use only "soul force," or *satyagraha*, the power of militant love. Gandhi first developed this method when he led South African "Indians" in protest against the pass laws.

Others argue that the nonviolent approach is *tactically* the only one to pursue. Although Archbishop Desmond Tutu is not an absolute pacifist, he believes the use of nonviolence can avoid a bloody civil war. By talking both with the African nationalist movements and their enemy, the President of South Africa, he hopes to find a negotiated solution.

For over fifty years, up until 1960, nonviolent actions were the sole tactics used by the African National Congress. Only after the Sharpeville Massacre of 1960 did the ANC conclude that nonviolent means had not been enough (See Chapter Six.) At that point, the ANC decided on the use of "armed struggle" as a tactic, beginning with attacks on physical structures. It was clear that these attacks were primarily symbolic, a form of "armed propaganda" to keep up the morale of the oppressed. Today, the ANC has broadened its permissible targets to include military and police personnel. Township violence against collaborators or suspected informers is not sanctioned but neither is it condemned.

Quite aside from any commitment to nonviolence as a principle, those who are openly resisting apartheid from inside the country cannot afford to espouse revolutionary violence as means to end tyranny unless they are prepared to pay for their words with a prison term or death. Church leaders who supported the Call to Prayer were quite clear that they were not calling for the violent overthrow of the government.

Even pacifists may defend themselves

The ANC often describes its use of force as a means of defending the black townships against foreign military occupation. Even Gandhi eventually accepted the principle that physical force can be used in self-defense. While he preferred *satyagraha*, he acknowledged the "Fascist exception" and saw that military force was necessary to defeat the Axis powers in World War II. (*Satyagraha* presupposes that the enemy has a conscience and a sense of compassion and mercy to which love can appeal.)

Absolute pacifists often refer to Jesus' commandment to turn the other cheek and to love the enemy unreservedly. The Sermon on the Mount, however, goes further. It calls for complete non-resistance to evil-doers (Matthew 5:39-41). To take such a commandment literally is to take up the cross in the path of the Messiah. A great many Christians, however, believe that Christ died for all and that this sacrifice has already accomplished salvation; it is not to be repeated literally.

In following Christ, Christians are called to love their enemies. We are not to act from a spirit of revenge and blind anger but to be led by a love that includes the interests and good of all. Sometimes in situations where all options fall short of goodness and all choices involve some form of coercion, active resistance to evil may be the more loving choice. If, for example, an armed burglar invades one's home in the middle of the night, is it better to try to talk to him, seeking to understand his point of view and background and offering him unreserved love regardless of personal risk, or is it better to disarm the robber using whatever force is necessary? Or ought one to call the police? In deciding what to do, one has to weigh one's responsiblity for the lives of others. The presence of vulnerable younger or older people in the house, for example, has to be considered. To sacrifice oneself by submitting to evil becomes a knottier problem when non-resistance means the possible sacrifice of others as well.

When facing grave injustice or a tyrannical government that is slaughtering innocent people, most Christians have felt compelled to resist rather than passively to submit to such massive social evil. To resist often means to use some coercion or force while striving to keep the amount used to a minimum. Most Christians do not believe that Matthew 5:39a requires that at all times, in all places and in all circumstances a Christian must submit to evil rather than resist it.

The question of whether Christians can support the work of the resistance and liberation movements in southern Africa turns on the question of whether a person may, under those exceptional circumstances, turn to the use of force as the lesser of two evils.[15]

Open and hidden violence

Violence has become a loaded word. When using the word, we must be aware of the bias that may be attached to it. To condemn without reservation whatever anyone chooses to call violence, as church leaders often do, ignores how the government of South Africa and the media use the term.

Usually, the media and the apartheid government use "violence" to refer to the actions of people in the black townships as they throw stones, burn cars and buildings and, sometimes, kill government collaborators. When gold miners go on strike, "violence" usually refers to their use of force against strikebreakers. But when the government acts to pass discriminatory laws or the army removes people from their homes by force or the police detain them without charges, the word used is not "violence" but the less frightening term, "repression." Actions of the armed forces are often criticized as "excessive" or as "misconduct" but not as "violent." We hear about "unrest" among South African blacks. What is the implication? That blacks should normally be at peace and at rest? The ANC is often described as a rebel group. Does this imply that it is rebelling against a legitimate government?

Often the violence of Africans against Africans is called "tribal fighting." More often what is happening is a clash between those who are fighting against apartheid and those who have become a part of it. One example is the fight between a large Zulu movement called *Inkatha* led by the head of the Zulu "homeland," Chief Gatsha Buthelezi, and supporters of the African National Congress and the United Democratic Front. For example, Buthelezi has used his Inkatha para-military squads to harass Durban townships that resist being incorporated into his homeland, has created rival labor unions in opposition to COSATU and has attacked ANC and UDF supporters. "Tribal" is not the correct term for this struggle of militant opponents of apartheid against a homeland leader who criticizes apartheid but inevitably collaborates with it by being part of the system.[16]

By using "violence" indiscriminately, we confuse the issue. By making a blanket condemnation of all violence, we mingle together situations that need to be considered separately: the actions of people to defend themselves, and the actions of a ruthless military force against them. Throughout the Bible, "violence" is used to describe the actions of evil and oppressive people. (For example, see Psalm 72:12-24; Isaiah 59:1-8; Jeremiah 22:13-17). "Violence" is not the word used to describe Israel's army as it attempts to defend Israel. Nor is "violence" used to describe Yahweh's action against the chariots and soldiers of Pharaoh's army as Yahweh liberates Israel from slavery.

Can a revolution be just?

Reflecting on years of discussion with European church leaders about this question, South African theologian Gabiel Setiloane has said:

> . . .The official Christian view, flung judgmentally at African revolutionaries and their sympathizers, was that a violent uprising against a state, no matter how immoral and iniquitous, was un-Christian and ungodly. We Africans had never really felt so. . . . [17]

Some Christians now argue that the southern African situation has passed the point where reform is possible. Therefore, a revolution is needed to replace the apartheid system with a new order, although this revolution will not necessarily require the use of violence. Others claim that even the use of violence cannot be excluded if a revolution is justified. Since Christians have used a "just war" theory to justify participation in World War II and other wars, why cannot a similar theory be applied to a civil war against a tyranny? Accordingly, they have developed a "just revolution" theory that has become more controversial than the "just war" reasoning.

In both theories six basic requirements must be met for war or revolution to be considered just. Some of these have to do with a just *resort* to war, others with the just *conduct* of war.

1. Legitimate authority. In order for a revolution to be just, the English theologian J.G. Davies argues, a sizeable proportion of the population must place its trust in the resistance movement. Usually it is a small group that first perceives the need for a revolution, but awareness of that need must become widespread if a revolution is to be successful. As Thomas Jefferson and the American revolutionaries argued, the people are the ultimate source of legitimate authority. Of course, Christians owe primary obedience to God and must look beyond popular opinion to find what is right. Recognition of this ultimate necessity to follow conscience has led many who cannot themselves side with a revolution to support the right of others to choose it as. This is the position of some South African church leaders today.

2. Just Cause. When a government fails to remove root causes of injustice and violently suppresses criticism and peaceful protest, when it brutalizes its citizens by killing them in cold blood or detaining without trial and torturing persons suspected of political activities, when its structural forms of violence amount to genocide, when it always rules in the interests of a minority, that government has become a tyranny. Against such unjust rule, submission and patient endurance may in the long run bring more severe physical and spiritual harm to more people than using force to end suffering would do. Mere biological survival cannot be the supreme value. Much of the evil that Hitler and Stalin did could have been avoided if forceful resistance had been taken earlier.

3. Last resort. When every effort to negotiate peaceful solutions has been habitually rebuffed for decades, and when the vast majority of people find their very lives and those of their children threatened, then resort to force may be right. Where legally sanctioned ways of conflict resolution exist, patience and evolution may be preferable. But sometimes force is the only language that an oppressor can hear.

4. Just goals. Wanting to end starvation and systemic violence is not enough. To be just, a revolution must have reasonable, careful and practical plans for changing conditions and establishing a more just and equal society. Obviously no revolution will usher in a utopia, but revolutions cannot simply aim to destroy the old order and its adherents. A just revolution must intend to preserve some of the old order and fuse it with new: it must care about reconciliation and be prepared to establish peace.

5. Just means. A just revolution implies that limits will be imposed on the kind and extent of violence used. Indiscriminate violence, particularly against people who are not involved in the army, the police or the administration of the system, cannot be justified and is in fact counterproductive. Just as few people today try to justify the slaughter of innocent civilians by saturation bombings or nuclear bombs in World War II, so it is hard to justify the use of gasoline-filled tires by militants to execute persons suspected of being "sellouts" in African townships. Arbitrary violence, terroristic acts and cruelty nullify any conceivable good that may be imagined to come from them.

6. Likely success, or proportionality. To be just, a revolution must do more good than harm. In some cases the amount of suffering through injustice and tyranny is great enough to outweigh the evils involved in the use of force. On the other hand, an unsuccessful revolution may involve much too much suffering to be worth it. What can we say about the enormous suffering imposed on the people of Mozambique, Angola, Namibia and South Africa by the present *kragdadigheit* regime? Can we condemn on principle planned resistance to such oppression—if on balance such resistance offers a reasonable chance of achieving freedom from oppression and a more just and democratic order?

Although no one can foretell the consequences of a successful revolution, there must be a reasonable chance that the change from the old order to the new can be achieved by military and political action. The forces of resistance must engage in accurate and realistic planning, military strategy, political acumen, diplomatic skill and persuasion of world opinion.

If the revolution does not maintain the relationship between the fight being waged and what is likely to be achieved, it loses whatever justification it had. Only the achievement of greater justice and freedom, the restoration of good government under God, and respect for fundamental laws and rights can justify an armed uprising. If the aim is simply to elevate another class of tyrants to power, the revolution is no more than murder.[18]

The Kairos

A crisis is shaking the foundations of apartheid. A critical and decisive break with the past is at hand for South Africa, a fullness of time when God's loving purpose will be realized, a *kairos*, to use the Greek word with which we began this book. A *kairos* offers a unique opportunity for repentance and conversion. It is a time of judgment and decision, a moment of truth when an old tyrannical order is so challenged that liberation comes for its victims.

This is the argument made by some of South Africa's church leaders in a bold paper called the *Kairos Document*, first published in September 1985.[19] The experience of laypeople and clergy groups engaged in the African townships produced this prophetic theology addressed to the churches.

The document opens with a challenge to "state theology," defined as a theological approach that justifies the status quo with its "racism, capitalism and totalitarianism." By misinterpreting Romans 13, state theology accords absolute authority to law and order—as if any law and order, no matter how abominable, had divine status. The *Kairos Document* sets forth a different view:

> [The god invoked by the new apartheid constitution] is an idol. It is as mischievous, sinister and evil as any of the idols that the prophets of Israel had to contend with. Here we have a God who is historically on the side of the white settlers, who dispossesses black people of their land and who gives the major part of the land to his "chosen people." It is the God of superior weapons ... casspirs and hippos [armed personnel carriers], teargas, rubber bullets, sjamboks [whips], prison cells and death sentences. . . . It is the devil disguised as Almighty God—the anti-Christ. [See the *Kairos Document*, Second Edition, Section 2.4, page 7]

On the other hand, what the authors call "church theology," which is typically enunciated by leaders of the English-speaking churches, would solve the apartheid problem by relying on a few stock ideas taken from the Christian tradition and applied superficially. Typically, such church leaders say:

> We must be fair. We must listen to both sides of the story. If the two sides can only meet to talk and negotiate, they will sort out their differences and misunderstandings, and the conflict will be resolved. [Section 3.1, p. 9]

The *Kairos Document* criticizes this approach as a mistaken application of the Christian doctrine of reconciliation: it confuses the means appropriate to settle a private quarrel with those appropriate to a conflict between an armed, aggressive oppressor and its unarmed, defenseless victims.

> In our situation . . . it would be totally unChristian to plead for reconciliation and peace before the present injustices have been removed. Any such plea plays into the hands of the oppressor by trying to persuade those of us who are oppressed to accept our oppression and to become reconciled to the intolerable crimes that are committed against us. That is not Christian reconciliation, it is sin. . . . No reconcilia-

tion is possible in South Africa without justice, without the total dismantling of apartheid.

What this means in practice is that no reconciliation, no forgiveness and negotiations are possible *without repentance*. [Section 3.1, p. 10]

When "church theology" talks about justice, it speaks of the justice of reform that will be brought about when the white minority, the oppressor, decides to make some concessions.

At the heart of this approach is the reliance upon "individual conversions" in response to "moralizing demands" to change the structures of society. It has not worked and it never will. . . . The problem we are dealing with here in South Africa is not merely a problem of personal guilt, it is a problem of structural injustice. [Section 3.2, p. 12]

God's justice, true justice, the document urges, demands not simply a change of heart but a change of structures. Given history and present attitudes, this change can come only "from below," from the oppressed themselves, as it did from the Hebrew slaves in Egypt.

To replace theologies that justify the state or promote a false reconciliation, the *Kairos Document* calls for a "prophetic theology." Such a theology will concentrate on aspects of the Word of God that speak to the situation of the oppressed, starting with their experience. A prophetic theology conveys hope for the future; it emboldens people to speak with courage and boldness; it confronts injustice with the spirit of the prophetic Christ; it names sin and calls for active measures to overcome it.

The *Kairos Document* appeals to the God of the Bible. For most of their history, the people of the Bible were oppressed by one ruler or another—from the pharaohs to the Assyrians and Babylonians, from the Romans to their own kings, ruling elders and high priests. The Psalms describe oppression vividly, as people cry out against being crushed (see Psalms 44, 94). But at the same time there is hope. Yahweh is revealed as the Holy One who is radically free, a liberator of those who suffer, a compassionate God who frees the poor from exploitation (see Psalm 74 and Exodus 3:7). As a liberator, God is not neutral. God does not attempt to reconcile Moses with Pharaoh, the slaves with their slave drivers.

Jesus took up the cause of the poor when he announced his mission in the words of Isaiah (Luke 4:18-19). Jesus called the rich and the oppressor to repentance. The oppressed Christians of South Africa feel united to Christ in their sufferings. He, too, was a victim of oppression and violence.

The *Kairos Document* argues that a tyrannical regime like the apartheid state is morally illegitimate and irreformable. Although Christians may differ about what means to use to replace it, "there can be no doubt about our Christian duty to refuse to co-operate with tyranny and to do whatever we can to remove it."

The center of the prophetic message must be hope, not bleak pessimism:

> Jesus has taught us to speak of this hope as the coming of God's kingdom. We believe that God is at work in our world turning hopeless and evil situations to good so that God's Kingdom may come and God's will may be done on earth as it is in heaven. We believe that goodness and justice and love will triumph in the end and that tyranny and oppression cannot last forever. [Section 4.5, p. 26]

The church needs to confirm the reality of God's power and love, which undergird and embrace the hopes of the people: "The people need to hear it said again and again that God is with them, and that the 'hope of the poor is never brought to nothing' (Psalm 9:18)." The oppressor, who is "desperately fearful," also needs to be given hope, but this cannot be the false hope of maintaining the status quo. The church must shed its neutrality, *Kairos* contends, and participate actively in peoples' campaigns, such as general strikes and consumer boycotts. "Ambulance ministry" is not enough. Worship services, education and other activities need to be reshaped to reflect the prophetic faith of the *kairos*. Yet in doing these things the church should steer clear of becoming a "third force" between oppressor and oppressed or becoming identified with one political party or ideology:

> . . . The church must not confuse the issue by having programs that run counter to the struggles of those political organizations that truly represent the grievances and the demands of the people. The church should be ready to disobey the state in order to obey God, avoiding giving any legitimacy to the apartheid government, even to the point of civil disobedience. [Section 5.4, p. 29]

Finally, the *Kairos Document* appeals to the worldwide fellowship of the church "to give us the necessary support in this regard so that the daily loss of so many young lives may be brought to a speedy end." [19]

Over 150 South African church leaders from 16 different denominations signed the *Kairos Document*. The response from the townships was "overwhelming excitement"; many welcomed it as a statement of what it means to be Christian under apartheid. A number of churches, Christian groups and individual theologians responded to it. Archbishop Tutu refused to sign because he felt that it caricatured the pioneering efforts of some church leaders and seemed to place "Pharaoh" beyond redemption and abandon dialogue. Some felt it paid insufficient attention to Africans' earlier efforts to develop their own theology as a protest against the racism of white missionaries. Some black theologians felt it was too "white" in orientation. A revised edition published in 1986 takes into account many early criticisms and elaborates the concept of "prophetic theology."

In an interesting parallel effort, a group of evangelicals published a devastating critique of the theology of their own evangelical denominations and of the charismatic and pentecostal movements. They especially deplored American conservative evangelicals like Jerry Falwell, who visited South Africa briefly and declared "apartheid has ended," and African evangelicals who curry favor from the rulers of apartheid.

> After declaring the State of Emergency on June 12, 1986, the South African TV replayed one North American evangelist's sermon. . . [in order] to justify the silencing of the oppressed majority . . . and declaring a news black-out to be able to kill and detain without being monitored. . . . [The sermon] called on South Africans to promote and defend so-called western civilization, western freedoms and democracy. Many black South Africans were outraged by this sermon and the arrogance of a foreigner who comes to tell us that apartheid is dead when we know that it is alive and well and that it kills.[20]

The "Concerned Evangelicals" attacked the conservative evangelical movement for using an obsession with what that movement calls the "threat of communism" as a reason to idolize capitalist culture, for attacking prophets who call for social change and for displaying extreme sectarian behavior and sometimes gross materialism.[21]

The road to Harare

Perhaps the most significant response to the *Kairos Document*
was the journey of South African church leaders to Harare,
Zimbabwe, in December 1985. They went at the invitation of the
World Council of Churches to meet with leaders of churches from
all over the world. There they urgently pled for understanding,
support and action at this critical moment in South Africa's history.
The Harare Declaration that issued from this conference boldly
picked up the challenge of the *Kairos Document*:

WE AFFIRM THAT THE MOMENT OF TRUTH (KAIROS)
IS NOW, BOTH FOR SOUTH AFRICA AND THE WORLD
COMMUNITY. We have heard the cries of the anguish of
the people of South Africa trapped in the oppressive
structures of apartheid. In this moment of immense
potentiality, we agree that the apartheid structure is against
God's will, and is morally indefensible. The South African
government has no credibility. We call for:
    —an end of the state of emergency,
    —the release of Nelson Mandela and all political prisoners,
    —the lifting of the ban on all banned movements,
    —the return of exiles.
The transfer of power to the majority of the people, based
on universal suffrage, is the only lasting solution to the
present crisis.

The Harare Declaration called on the churches to fast and pray
on the tenth anniversary of the Soweto uprising, June 16, 1986,
for an end to unjust rule. It called on the international community
not to extend, roll-over or renew bank loans to South Africa and
to apply immediate and comprehensive sanctions against South
Africa. It called on the churches inside and outside South Africa
to support the movements working for the country's liberation.

The participants at Harare then pledged that they would use
their own individual powers, influence, energies and offices to turn
what they had learned into programs of urgent action.[22]

Eighteen months later, representatives of churches, trade unions,
and women's, youth and anti-apartheid groups met in Lusaka,
Zambia, to review the situation since Harare. They concluded that,
while the situation in South Africa had worsened considerably,
the implementation of the Harare Declaration had not been as
vigorous as it might have been. The participants recognized that

the people of the African nations nearest to South Africa were being subjected to "overwhelming material sacrifice and suffering." And so they called for greater immediate assistance to the Southern African Development Coordination Conference and other agencies struggling to cope with economic dependence on South Africa, with South African refugees and with support for the liberation movements.

In addition, the Lusaka meeting condemned the United States for delaying Namibia's independence by linking to it the issue of the Cuban troops in Angola. Because of the censorship of the media in South Africa, the meeting urged the churches to take steps to make fair and objecting reporting of events in the region a reality. It also asked the WCC to monitor how the Harare and Lusaka resolutions are being carried out.[23]

Summing it up

In this chapter we have considered how we hear the Word of God so that it becomes a living source of liberation, renewal and strength. We have looked at questions and ideas that we bring to our reading of the Scriptures. Inevitably, the questions we ask of God and of the Bible reflect our situation. If we are privileged, comfortable, white and middle-class, we may find it difficult to understand how black Christians who live in African townships think about their life, how they approach questions of love and justice and reconciliation, and even how they understand God. Conversely, those who experience oppression find it difficult to understand the apathy and complacency of those who are not oppressed. Here we have tried to liberate our thinking from conventional wisdom derived from our own situations alone, from biases that may not be objective and from assumptions that may not be correct. If we have heard the challenge of prophetic theology from South Africa, we may now be feeling the tug of a call to action. What useful choices might we be able to make? In our last chapter, we will look at what we can do to answer the call of South Africa's oppressed people for help in their struggle.

Chapter Nine:

What Then Shall We Do?

Our children are dying. Our land is burning and bleeding and so I call upon the international community to apply punitive sanctions against this government. . . . I have no hope of real change from this government unless they are forced. We face a catastrophe in this land and only the action of the international community by applying pressure can save us. [Archbishop Desmond Tutu, April 2, 1986]

We have now seen apartheid in action and South African Christians caught up in suffering because of it. Those who suffer have challenged us to help them as "members one of another" within the body of Christ. They need our support. God calls us to translate our understanding of the issues into committed, faithful response to this *kairos*. Faith requires that we trust God to find a way. But it also requires us to offer our own faithful obedience: to search out specific ways to support those who suffer under oppression and struggle to end it. How shall we do this?

With One Voice!

In January 1986, church leaders from twenty-four U.S. denominations and twelve inter-church agencies, along with the National Council of Churches and the World Council of Churches U.S. Office, created the Churches' Emergency Committee on Southern Africa (CECSA). Their aim was to carry out the program of action against apartheid called for in the Harare Declaration of December 1985 (see page 150).

CECSA can already point to some accomplishments. On June 15, 1986, hundreds of Christians came to Washington, D.C., to worship, pray and lobby for comprehensive sanctions against South Africa. Three days later the House of Representatives unanimously passed a sweeping ban on all trade and investment. The final vote in October to enact selective sanctions by overriding a Presidential veto reflected the churches' organized efforts to have sanctions declared.* Partly as a result of church pressures for disinvestment, a number of U.S. businesses have announced that they are "pulling out" of South Africa. But much more remains to be done. Let us consider in detail how a denomination, a congregation, or concerned individuals might support South Africans struggling against apartheid.

Sanctions Legislation

Sanctions—legal withholding of commerce with one nation by another in order to press for change through an economic "squeeze"—are major tools that our governments have in relation to South Africa. Any advocacy of sanctions has to be understood in the context of existing Canadian and U.S. policy and practice toward South Africa.

Except for a largely ineffective arms embargo imposed on a voluntary basis against South Africa in 1962 and made mandatory in 1977, U.S. administrations have routinely dismissed sanctions as a method of bringing about change. Sanctions have been seen as an unwise interference with profitable trade and investment. Instead, over the last thirty years, these administrations have denounced apartheid when it was necessary to show that America's heart was in the right place. To promote change away from apartheid, the United States has relied on the possibility of a white change of heart, counting on "enlightened" Afrikaners to transform the system through gradual internal reforms. Black liberation movements have been viewed as counterproductive at best and, at worst, as leading to violence, revolution and communism.

In the 1980s, President Reagan has seen South Africa as a friend and ally of the United States. The Reagan administration has operated from a "war of two worlds" ideology like that South African government espouses (see Chapter 7, page 105.) This administration has set as a major U.S. goal the reversal of "the decline in security and stability [in southern Africa] which has been underway now since the early and mid 1970s." The violence in southern Africa, according to this view, is attributed to Cuba and the Soviet Union, not to South Africa's *kragdadigheit*. So stability is more likely to be realized by being friendly and encouraging, offering sympathetically couched advice to Pretoria ("carrots") rather than using sanctions ("sticks") to pressure for change.

---

* For explanation of sanctions, divestment and disinvestment, see note page 73.

Concessions on Namibia and internal reform in South Africa were to be brought about through "constructive engagement."[1]

Not unreasonably, South Africa understood these U.S. policies to mean that intransigence and aggression would be tolerated, not penalized. Friendly dialogue only proved to license and encourage South Africa's military rulers. The South African government refused to make concessions on Namibia or to execute internal reforms of any consequence. By 1985 the Reagan administration could show no fruits from its policy of "constructive engagement."

Until recently, Canadian governments have followed a similar policy of non-intervention in the free market interchange of goods, services and capital between Canada and South Africa. In 1985 and 1986, however, the Canadian government under Prime Minister Brian Mulroney began to enact sanctions in concert with the initiatives and positions of the rest of the Commonwealth nations. Canada has banned imports of South African agricultural products, steel, iron, coal, uranium and arms.

Despite the opposition of the Reagan administration, the United States Congress finally imposed a series of mild selective sanctions in October 1986. The United States law now bars the same imports that Canada does, plus imports of textiles, Krugerrand gold coins, and commodities produced by South African government parastatal corporations such as aluminum and cement. South Africa's sugar quota has been transferred to the Philippines. U.S. exports of petroleum products, crude oil, munitions and nuclear technology or materials are banned. Computers, software and services can no longer be exported to the South African military, police and other agencies administering apartheid. New public and private loans and investments from the U.S. are also forbidden by this law. South African Airways can no longer land in the United States nor can U.S. airlines serve South Africa.

While these selective sanctions are an important step toward ending Canadian and U.S. support for apartheid, loopholes in the laws and regulations permit South Africa to continue business as usual in many sectors of the economy. For example, short-term trade financing and rescheduling of existing debts are still permitted under the U.S. law. And while no new U.S. investments are to be made, profits from existing investments can be reinvested either in the corporation's own business in South Africa or in any other South African entity. Anyone in the United States can still invest in South African stocks and bonds. The U.S. administration has in effect nullified the ban on imports of uranium from South Africa and Namibia by creating a special regulation excepting it. Canada discourages new loans to the government of South Africa and the sale of Krugerrands, but compliance is still voluntary. In a number of other areas also Canada has not yet followed the recommendations which the Commonwealth countries adopted at a meeting in Nassau, the Bahamas, in October 1985.[2]

The United States' selective sanctions are part of a Comprehensive Anti-Apartheid law that takes a negative view of the African National Congress. The bill refers to the ANC as a "terrorist" organization and orders an investigation into its activities in the U.S. Furthermore, although military cooperation with South Africa is banned, intelligence cooperation with South Africa continues. The assumption behind these provisions is that the liberation movements are more responsible for the violence and instability in South Africa than is the apartheid government.

The case for comprehensive sanctions

1. Some argue that sanctions against South Africa have not worked because they have not immediately and directly brought about their announced goal. Yet history shows that sanctions can in fact have an important, if not immediate, effect in achieving change. Even unilateral and partial sanctions impose a toll over time and can help bring about change indirectly as well as directly, although the final outcome may differ from the announced goal.

Sanctions imposed by the United States against countries it considers are moving toward communism have been successful. In 1973, for example, U.S. sanctions against Chile were a major factor in overthrowing the government of Salvador Allende. A 1985 Institute of International Economics study concluded that sanctions had worked in 36 percent of the cases studied, including Chile, Rhodesia, Uganda and Iran.[3]

In the case of Rhodesia, the United Nations imposed sanctions in order to assist Great Britain, the colonial ruler of that country, to bring about a transfer of power from the white to the African majority. The sanctions were imposed only gradually and were only partially enforced by the nations that imposed them. International oil companies supplied Rhodesia with petroleum products via their South African subsidiaries. The U.S. Congress allowed "strategic" minerals to be imported from Rhodesia. Yet these sanctions imposed heavy costs on Rhodesia. "Sanctions busting" imports cost Rhodesia double the usual price. It was expensive to build up local industries, which could not make up for the lack of imported raw materials and capital equipment. Sanctions isolated Rhodesia diplomatically and politically. Only Portugal and South Africa supported the outlaw white government. When that support was withdrawn, Rhodesia had to come to terms with liberation movements that had gained in recognition and legitimacy from sanctions.[4]

2. Even though comprehensive sanctions stand a good chance of helping to bring about fundamental change in South Africa, it should be understood that this process will take a long time. At this moment South Africa stands defiant, as it has often done before. Sanctions are therefore not the *cause* of its hardline attitude. Nor should sanctions be considered a cheap, easy way to induce meaningful negotiations. That is the fantasy the British government promoted when it asked for sanctions against Rhodesia in 1965. Nevertheless, there is substantial evidence that, given sufficient time, the Rhodesian sanctions did work.

South Africa is in fact far more vulnerable to sanctions than Rhodesia was because it is much more dependent on imports of sophisticated technology. In addition, the South African economy is suffering from a severe economic crisis; Rhodesia was not when sanctions were first imposed.[5] Rhodesia had as its support the neighboring nation of South Africa with its sophisticated commercial facilities and its access to the sea, which could shield its trade from scrutiny; South Africa has no such neighbor.

The ultimate aim of sanctions is the negotiated surrender of power by the white supremacist regime so that a new, non-racist and democratic order may emerge. Nothing short of that aim will satisfy the hopes and desires of the vast majority of South Africans. At some point, negotiations *will* come about; as the 1986 report of the Commonwealth Eminent Persons Group shows, that the moment is not now.[5] Yet comprehensive, multilateral sanctions can hasten the day and, by making armed resistance less necessary, minimize the violence of the transition.

Sanctions are at least part of a nonviolent solution. What alternatives exist? It is clear that neither the United States nor Canada is prepared to end apartheid by sending troops. But it is equally clear from South African history that mere talking is not enough. To negotiate surrender of power will require a different balance of forces than now exists.

3. Sanctions do create some hardship and suffering, but this is the price of creating hope for real change. Sanctions will hurt the white regime more than blacks. The argument that sanctions will be most harmful to blacks is usually made by the South African government or by whites who have business interests in South Africa. Among prominent black political figures, only Chief Gatsha Buthelezi opposes sanctions, and as we have seen (see page 142), he has become more and more a part of the apartheid system.

At the 1985 Harare meeting, American church leaders were impressed with the power and urgency with which most South African church leaders spoke in favor of sanctions.[6]

Here are several reasons for thinking that sanctions will not necessarily be as harmful to blacks as opponents claim. (Some of these reasons also apply to divestment, to be considered later.)

- Black South Africans are asking for sanctions.
- South African companies taking over operations from foreign investors may well find that when they are deprived of technology and capital goods, they will have to substitute labor for capital, thus creating jobs for more black workers.
- Although South Africa has threatened to impose counter-sanctions against neighboring black nations, this retaliation may not prove to be in Pretoria's interests. Some of these nations are important markets for South African exports.
- If the nine independent, black-ruled countries of the Southern Africa Development Coordination Conference can achieve a greater measure of self-sufficiency by developing their own trade routes to the sea and by achieving greater self-development, then trade sanctions will not hurt them as much. To do so will require from European and American countries a clear commitment to making the SADCC plans work. And obviously, capital for such projects as the Beira Corridor is crucial (see page 121).

What about the argument that the white regime is largely invulnerable? Recall the analysis we have made of the South African economy. In fact, South Africa is far more vulnerable to sanctions than is generally admitted. The government greeted the imposition of selective sanctions with political frenzy. Foreign Minister Pik Botha telephoned U.S. senators and threatened to cut off imports of American grain if the Congress imposed sanctions. Allister Sparks, who reports for the *Washington Post* from

South Africa, comments on whites' vulnerability to economic pressures:

> One didn't hear many cries of distress coming from Soweto the other day when the Rand crashed to 34 U.S. cents. . . . But the reactions from the other side of the apartheid track suggests that for all its vaunted resilience, white South Africa, spoiled by years of affluence and privilege, has a very low threshold of tolerance of economic pain.[7]

4. Some who argue against sanctions point to the unanimity of Afrikaner opinion. Sanctions, it is sometimes argued, will drive the Afrikaner rulers of South Africa further into their *laager* (the defensive circle of pioneer trekker wagons).

But the present situation indicates that the Afrikaner consensus is in fact breaking down. On the extreme right, some Afrikaner groups are attacking the government for selling out whites. On the moderate edge of the Nationalist party, political figures like Dennis Worrall, a former government minister, have run for Parliament as independents. A leading liberal Afrikaner politician, Van Zyl Slabbert, has resigned from Parliament because conventional white politics cannot find a solution to the crisis. In 1987 Slabbert led a delegation of some sixty Afrikaners from all walks of life to Senegal to discuss the possibilities for a solution with the African National Congress.

A number of distinguished Afrikaner theologians like Beyers Naudé criticize apartheid as a heresy and have called for sanctions. Many white church leaders signed the *Kairos Document*. The number of whites who are dissatisfied with apartheid is growing. Many young white people are not turning up to do their military service. Some go abroad or find jobs overseas rather than live under apartheid. The loss of professional skills to the nation is substantial.[8]

5. Many church people have supported fair employment codes for U.S. and Canadian businesses operating in South Africa as a step more positive than sanctions. But after ten years of trying to practice these codes, it is clear that the codes have done nothing to change the apartheid system. They cannot be effectively monitored; they affect only a tiny fraction of the work force; and they do not deal with the central issue of political rights.

After ten years of promoting such a code—the plan was known internationally by his name—the prominent American black church leader, Leon Sullivan, announced in June 1987 that corporations should pull out of South Africa and that the United States should cut off all South African trade and sever diplomatic relations until apartheid is ended. Sullivan said:

> In spite of our efforts, the main pillars of apartheid remain and blacks are still denied basic civil rights. Repression against blacks grows. People are brutalized. The government's intransigence to fundamental change continues.[9]

Other legislative issues

Implementation of Resolution 435. It is now almost ten years since the United Nations Security Council adopted Resolution 435 setting up a plan for the independence of Namibia (see page 113). But South Africa's refusal to cooperate in implementing the resolution has made it for now a dead letter. The churches of Namibia have condemned the "unholy alliance between the United States and the Republic of South Africa" in bypassing the resolution and linking Namibian independence to extraneous issues like the presence of Cuban troops in Angola. Urge your legislators to put pressure on the United States and Canadian governments to implement Resolution 435.

Aid to SADCC. In 1980, when the nine independent, black-ruled countries of southern Africa formed the Southern Africa Development Coordination Conference (SADCC), they began to create a regional development plan to reduce dependency on South Africa and other external powers and to increase investment, mutual trade and interdependence within the region.

International funding is necessary to implement these plans. It is important that this funding not be given on a country-by-country approach but on a basis that respects the joint decisions which the countries of the region have made. Priorities for funding are transport and communications, agricultural research and food security, alternative energy sources, and industrial development.

Aid to UNITA. It is important to press U.S. legislators to stop providing military aid to the UNITA movement, which is headed by Jonas Savimbi and aided extensively by South Africa (see page 115). Under U.S. law, all military and para-military aid to anti-government forces in Angola was prohibited by the Clark Amendment of 1976, but Congress repealed this ban in 1985. That prohibition should be restored; to oppose apartheid means to take seriously what the South African government does against its neighbors to protect apartheid at home.

Millions of dollars worth of sophisticated American-made equipment is sent to help UNITA carry on its war against the Angolan government. No African government in the region supports this aid, with the possible exception of Zaire, which in the past has allowed the CIA to use its territory for supplying UNITA. The Organization of African Unity and the SADCC nations have both condemned these actions of the United States.

Support for UNITA will be very costly to the people of Angola and to the region, warns Simbarashi Makoni, the executive secretary of SADCC:

> There will be no development, no stability, no western democracy, no free enterprise system to talk about. It will only result in further suffering for the poor people of Angola. Is it of greater American interest that we should keep [Angolan] peasants destitute and suffering in order to stop "Soviet expansionism"?[10]

The United Church of Christ and the United Methodist Church, which have important mission links to Angola, have opposed aid to UNITA.

How can citizens influence their legislators.

The Washington Office on Africa (WOA) is an indispensable office for U.S. Christians to be in touch with (see general information section which follows for address). It provides information about the current legislation, information packets on various issues and valuable analysis of what is happening in South Africa and the region. WOA is sponsored by several Protestant denominations and Roman Catholic orders, the American Committee on Africa and three U.S. trade unions.

In Canada you should be in touch with the Task Force on the Churches and Corporate Responsibility (see general information section). The Task Force's Annual Report for 1985-1986 contains recommendations for strengthening Canada's existing sanctions program.

Experience indicates that the most effective way to influence a legislator is to meet with him or her face-to-face, in a group if possible, and to lay out your concerns simply, clearly and in your own words. Tell the legislator what you think is desirable:

"Please support Bill Number ——(citing its title and principal sponsors)," or "We would appreciate your taking this position." Be patient and courteous but firm. Listen carefully to what the legislator has to say. If possible, commend the legislator for a previous vote, speech or position taken. Thank him or her for the time spent with you. Follow up your visit with a letter summarizing what you said and any verbal commitment the legislator made.

Many legislators keep office hours in their local districts, so it is not always necessary to go to the national capital to lobby for what you want.

Personal, thoughtful letters also play an important role in influencing legislators. A one-page letter on a single topic is more effective than a longer one that tries to cover all of the issues you are concerned about. Your congregation may need a form letter to start thoughts flowing or a general outline of points to be made. Form letters signed in bulk or petitions are less effective unless they are produced in massive numbers. Mention positions that your church or denomination has taken on apartheid sanctions, Namibia, aid to UNITA or whatever the topic is.

Divestment

For a long time, the anti-apartheid movement in the United States, Canada and other countries has recognized the key role played by multinational corporations in propping up apartheid. Hard campaigning over the years has built momentum as the crisis in South Africa has deepened. By 1987, 19 states, 70 cities and 116 universities in the United States and many similar bodies in Canada, together with many religious organizations, foundations and labor unions had adopted measures mandating divestment of all shares held in companies doing business in South Africa or had taken such other economic actions as boycotting products of companies continuing to operate in South Africa.

What began as a trickle has become a mighty flood of citizen action. Without these divestment and selective purchasing campaigns, it is doubtful that U.S. Congress or the Canadian government would have enacted any sanctions. Without citizen action, the various "withdrawals" by such U.S. corporations such as IBM, Kodak, General Motors and Coca-Cola would not have occurred, even though many companies allege purely business reasons for moving out. It is important, however, to ask whether the reality of withdrawal matches the public declaration. The model of a genuine withdrawal is Eastman Kodak, which has simply renounced all further business dealings with South Africa.

Other companies, despite apparent and announced withdrawal, continue to provide vital economic support through ongoing licensing, distribution, marketing and service agreements.

If your church or denomination has agreed to divest or is considering divestment, the following criteria are important. This list has been developed by the leading organizations in the Campaign Against Investment in South Africa.

A corporation is doing business in South Africa or Namibia if it, its parent or its subsidiaries:

—have direct investments in South Africa or Namibia, or have entered into franchise, licensing or management agreements with or for any entity in those countries; or

—are financial institutions that have not prohibited new investments, loans, credits or related services, or renewal of existing financial agreements, including those for the purposes of trade, with any entity in those countries; or

—have more than 5 percent of their common stock beneficially owned or controlled by a South African entity.

(These rules do not apply to companies that are in South Africa or Namibia simply to report news.)

Further information about divestment questions can be obtained from the following members of the Campaign Against Investment in South Africa:

American Committee on Africa
American Friends Service Committee
Clergy and Laity Concerned
Interfaith Center on Corporate Responsibility
TransAfrica
United Methodist Office for the United Nations
Washington Office on Africa

For addresses and telephone numbers see information section below.

The Investor Responsibility Research Center, 1755 Massachusetts Avenue, N.W., Washington, DC 20036 (telephone: 202-939-6500) investigates divestment issues for U.S. universities and other institutional investors.

For information on divestment questions concerning Canadian corporations and other Canadian issues, you may want to consult the Task Force on the Churches and Corporate Responsibility (see general information section for address and telephone number.)

Demonstrations and civil disobedience

One of the clearest signs of public disapproval of apartheid has been the massive protests and demonstrations orchestrated by the Free South Africa Movement and local coalitions in the United States and Canada. Standing outside the South African Embassy and its consulates as well as outside U.S. and Canadian corporation offices, demonstrators show their solidarity with those who are fighting apartheid inside the country. A number of volunteers occasionally do such acts of civil disobedience as violating police rules against entering the embassy.

By making visible protests both against apartheid and against policies that condemn apartheid without supporting effective comprehensive sanctions, protestors keep the issues in the public eye. This kind of publicity is an indispensable ingredient in the effort to get legislation enacted and policy changed.

The Call to Conscience Emergency Response Network responds to politically significant events in South Africa or the United States by issuing calls for public action to regional, state and local groups. It is coordinated by the American Friends Service Committee, Southern Africa Program (see general information section).

Protest demonstrations or events in your region or city usually will be coordinated by a coalition of groups, some secular and some religious. One example of such demonstration in the U.S. was the National Mobilization for Justice and Peace in Central America and Southern Africa, held during one long weekend in April 1987. A rally and march on Saturday were followed by interfaith worship on Sunday and nonviolent civil disobedience and lobbying the U.S. Congress on Monday.

Pray for liberation

On June 16, 1985 and 1986, people throughout South Africa prayed for the removal of "the tyrannical structures of oppression and the unjust rulers in our country" (see page 129). Those who prayed asked people of goodwill all over the world to join with them. So is particularly appropriate that throughout the Christian world special services of worship be designed for a "South Africa Sunday." These services can bring together our concerns for our brothers and sisters in South Africa, especially remembering all who have died in the struggle for a new and just society. If possible, choose a date that both fits your church's worship calendar and is significant in South African history: June 16 is the anniversary of Soweto and its martyrs; March 21 is the anniversary of the massacre at Sharpeville; June 26 is the anniversary of the day the Freedom Charter was adopted. If a South African pastor is available, ask him or her to preach. Your denominational offices may help you arrange for a speaker. Episcopal Churchpeople for a Free Southern Africa often have current information on church people who have been detained or have witnessed recent events in South Africa (see information section). A helpful selection of rituals and readings is *Torch in the Night: Worship Resources from South Africa* (see inside back cover).

Pray for those who suffer

In addition to designing a special service for a South Africa Sunday, include your concerns for the people of South Africa in your individual and corporate intercessions. Pray regularly and systematically for the churches and other religious bodies of South Africa, that they may be brave and faithful to their calling. Pray particularly for the people of the denomination with which your congregation is affiliated.

Include in your personal and corporate prayers the names of those who are in any kind of trouble, need or danger in South Africa. Hundreds of churchpeople, both lay and clergy, have been detained without trial or imprisoned for their convictions. Some are restricted by "banning orders," a kind of house arrest. Current lists can be obtained from Episcopal Churchpeople for a Free Southern Africa, Amnesty International or your denomination.

Protest detentions, write to detainees

In addition to praying, it is important to *communicate* your love, solidarity and support for persons suffering persecution, especially those in prison or detention, by showing your understanding and support in writing:

—to the person in prison or detention;
—to the person's family and relatives; and
—to President P.W. Botha
    Union Buildings, Pretoria 0001, South Africa

Send copies to your legislative representatives, to the President or the Prime Minister, and to the State Department or the Canadian Ministry of Foreign Affairs.

The Detainees' Parents Support Committee (at P.O. Box 39431, Bramley 2018, Johannesburg, South Africa) and the Black Sash (Khotso House, 42 De Villiers Street, Johannesburg 2001, South Africa) are two organizations that work for and with detainees and political prisoners. Both are worth supporting.

In the U.S., the Southern Africa Project of the Lawyers Committee for Civil Rights under Law works to support the legal defense of political prisoners (see information section for address).

Another group that works with political prisoners is Amnesty International. You can get in touch with the Southern Africa Coordination Group through Suzanne Riveles (9007 Garland Avenue, Silver Spring, MD 20901) or Mort Winston (507 East 39th Street, Baltimore, MD 21218).

For an example of how important this kind of support work can be, consider the case of Simon Tshenuweni Farisani, who was released from detention in the Venda homeland on January 30, 1987. Here is the story of how various groups advocated his release, as told by the Namibia Communications Centre in London:

> Church sources reported today that the Rev. Simon Thsenuweni Farisani, a dean of the Evangelical Lutheran Church in South Africa, has been on hunger strike since January 1, in protest at his continued detention . . . in Venda, an "independent homeland". . . .
>
> Farisani has been detained three times in recent years. During his last detention . . . he was tortured extensively and suffered two heart attacks.
>
> Mrs. Regina Farisani said in a telephone interview today the authorities have denied her access to her husband. . . . Mrs. Farisani appealed to the International Red Cross to visit her husband, so that pressure could be brought to insure his safety. . . .
>
> Farisani is well known in Europe, North America and Asia through his activities on behalf of Amnesty International. . . . Amnesty officials have called for Farisani's unconditional release, and have issued an urgent action bulletin to their members. . . . Lutheran churches around the world are also pressuring the Venda and South African authorities. . . . An

extensive letter writing campaign on his behalf has been
carried out in the United States. . . .

Dean Farisani has been an articulate spokesman against
the South African government. . . . "Our lives are in the hands
of the Lord," says Regina Farisani.

Material aid to the liberation movements

Not all blacks who are in exile from South Africa are involved
in guerilla warfare. For every one who is involved in fighting,
there are twenty who are simply refugees, often living in very
cramped and barren conditions. In Angola, for example, the
liberation movement of the Namibian people, SWAPO, runs a
refugee camp for Namibians under the supervision of the United
Nations High Commissioner for Refugees. In this camp live as
many as 70,000 women, children, youth and old people who have
fled from the war. The African National Congress runs camps,
educational schools and other training institutions for South
African exiles in Zambia and Tanzania. In Zimbabwe and in South
Africa there are many Mozambican refugees who have fled from
the fighting between the Mozamibique National Resistance (MNR),
backed by South Africa, and the Mozambican and Zimbabwean
armies. The South African Council of Churches and the Zimbabwe
Christian Council are ministering to the needs of these refugees.

If you want to help these refugees, get in touch with the National
Council of Churches USA, Church World Service, the Canadian
Council of Churches, the Lutheran World Federation or the Africa
Fund of the American Commitee on Africa and they will be able
to help you choose or contribute to a worthwhile project (for
addresses see general information section).

There may be projects inside South Africa which your
denomination can suggest to you. Develop your own criteria for
what kind of project will truly advance the transformation of South
Africa into a just, democratic and non-racist society.

Be creative in fund-raising. An example: members of a United
Methodist Church in Sudbury, Massachussetts, decided to sell their
family diamonds, since diamonds are mined in South Africa, as
a protest against apartheid. Their pastor, Gwen Purushotham,
began by putting her ring in the offering plate saying, "We give
this ring for the glory of God and the liberation of God's people."
The $5,000 raised by selling the diamonds will go to a Methodist
Resource and Reconciliation Center in Johannesburg.

Helping the Trade Union Movement

For information about how you can best help a trade union inside South Africa, you may get in touch with:

—The Coalition of Black Trade Unionists
c/o William Lucy, The American Federation of State,
County and Municipal Employees (AFSCME)
1625 L Street, N.W., Washington, DC 20036

—United Mine Workers
900 15th Street, N.W., Washington, DC 20005

UMW maintains a liaison with the National Union of Mineworkers in South Africa, an important element in the Confederation of South African Trade Unions (COSATU). They also coordinate a boycott of Shell Oil, which has a bad labor record in the United States and Canada as well as in South Africa.

Staying informed and informing the public

Now that the South African government has clamped down on all reporting from South Africa, it is all the more important for us and our churches to take the lead in spreading public knowledge about apartheid. Such knowledge will help correct the false propaganda that is spread through various channels, including some religious groups. You may want to get detailed, reliable news from South Africa and Namibia by subscribing to:

—*The Namibian*, P.O. Box 20783, Windhoek 9000, Namibia

—*The Weekly Mail*, P.O. 260425, Excom 2023, South Africa

—*The New Nation*, P.O. Box 10674, Johannesburg 2000, South Africa

—*Southscan*, 31 Washington Street, Brooklyn, NY 11201

Episcopal Churchpeople for a Free Southern Africa (see information section) reprints significant articles. A number of churches in South Africa publish their own newspapers. *Africa News* (P.O. Box 3851, Durham, NC 27702) is an important biweekly journal of objective news from all over the continent.

Be sure to write letters to the editor of your local newspaper to express your point of view. Make known your opposition to apartheid and to slanted or biased news about Africa. Be an advocate for sanctions. Usually your community radio or television station will be glad to consider scheduling program time for a visiting South African or Namibian who has been involved in the churches' struggle for a just society. Don't forget to call in and express your point of view on talk shows.

Films and audio visual resources

Most of us get a great deal of our information about the world visually. You may find a film or videotape a good way to understand the crisis in South Africa better. In *Until We Are Free*, the study guide for this book, you will find a list of films on the crisis in South Africa. Other lists of good films available for rental or purchase can be obtained from: Southern Africa Media Center, California Newsreel, 630 Natoma Street, San Francisco, CA 94103 (telephone: 415-621-6196). A "Guide to Films on Apartheid and the Southern Africa Region" and a listing of distributors are also available from Media Network, 208 West 13th Street, New York, NY 10011.

Books

Those who want to pursue further some of the issues discussed in this book will find at the end of this chapter a list of some useful books. See also the inside back cover. An additional bibliography is found in the study guide, *Until We Are Free*.

Speakers

Church leaders from South Africa and Southern Africa frequently visit the United States and Canada. A speaking tour may be arranged for your region. During the spring of 1987, for example, the Africa Peace Tour visited the southern U.S., bringing people from Africa and experts on Africa to speak in local communities. Local coalitions often need volunteers to help in arranging publicity, local media contacts, transportation and speaking engagements.

Your congregation might be able to arrange for a South African or Namibian church worker from your own denomination to be temporarily "in residence" on your church's staff. Through your denominational offices you may be able to get in touch with a South African or Namibian Christian who is studying in a seminary, university or school in your area. Exchanges of information and views in a relaxed and extended time together can be highly productive.

General Information

For up-to-date information on South Africa, Namibia and anti-apartheid movement, call or write to:

—The American Committee on Africa/The Africa Fund
198 Broadway, New York, NY 10038   (212-962-1210).
Founded in 1952, ACOA has been prominent in anti-apartheid work for years; special emphasis on divestment; written resources on sanctions and divestment issues.

—American Friends Service Committee Southern Africa Program
1501 Cherry Street, Philadelphia, PA 19102   (215-241-7169)
A activist Quaker organization working on divestment, sanctions and other nonviolent methods through regional network. Coordinates joint meetings of groups doing anti-apartheid work.

—Africa Resource Center
464 19th Street, Oakland, CA 94612   (415-763-8011)
A West Coast public library, speakers bureau and literature center on Africa.

—African National Congress of South Africa
801 Second Avenue, Room 405
New York, NY 10017   (212-490-3487)
The oldest and most prominent South African liberation movement; provides information and speakers.

—Canadian Council of Churches: see Interchurch Coalition on Africa.

—Churches' Emergency Committee on Southern Africa
475 Riverside Drive, Room 612
New York, NY 10115   (212-678-0969)
Responsible for implementation of the Harare Declaration and subsequent efforts. Works out of the Africa Office of the National Council of Churches.

—Church Women United
777 United Nations Plaza, Room 10E, New York, NY 10017
Ecumenical organization of women on justice and peace.

—Church World Service
475 Riverside Drive
New York, NY 10115   (212-870-3042)
Deals with issues concerning and support of refugees, displaced persons and returnees, including refugees in southern Africa. CWS

is the relief and development agency of the National Council of
Churches.

—Clergy and Laity Concerned
198 Broadway, New York, NY 10038   (212-964-6730)
An activist ecumenical coalition on a number of international issues.

—Council of Churches in Namibia, CCN
P.O. Box 41
Windhoek 9000, Namibia   (Country code 264 : 61-37510)

—Episcopal Church People for a Free Southern Africa
339 Lafayette Street, New York, NY 10012   (212-447-0066).
Publishes frequent bulletins of current information, news, detentions,
persecutions, strikes, church statements. Namibia a special interest.

—Interchurch Coalition on Africa
129 St. Clair Ave., West
Toronto, Ontario, M4V 1N5 Canada (416-927-1124)
Part of the Canadian Council of Churches; provides educational
material for church use on southern Africa.

—Interfaith Center for Corporate Responsibility
475 Riverside Drive, Room 566,
New York, NY 10115   (212-870-2293).
Coordinates corporate responsibility campaigns of a number of
denominations and religious orders, specializing in annual meeting
resolutions, divestment issues.

—International Defense and Aid Fund
P.O. Box 17, Cambridge, MA 02238, and
P.O. Box 1034, Station B, Ottawa, Ontario, Kl P 541, Canada
Human rights issues, pamphlets, books, information.

—Lawyers Committee South Africa Project
1400 Eye Street N.W., Suite 400
Washington, DC 20005   (202-371-1212).
Support for legal challenges to apartheid, political prisoners, legal
research on South Africa.

—Lutheran World Ministries
360 Park Ave. South, New York, NY 10010   (212-532-6350)
Publishes materials on Namibia, where Lutherans are a majority of
the population; refugee support.

—National Council of Churches Africa Office,
Division of Overseas Ministries, Room 612,
475 Riverside Drive, New York, NY 10115-0050   (212-870-2645)

Responsible for coordinating support for the work of African churches, including development, training and communication.

—National Namibia Concerns
860 Emerson Street, Denver, CO 80218
Network for action, information, and education on Namibia issues. Scholarships for Namibians.

—South African Council of Churches (SACC)
P.O. Box 4921, Johannesburg 2000,
Republic of South Africa   (Country Code 27 : 11-28-22511/8).
Leading ecumenical organization in South Africa; offers publications and information.

—SWAPO
801 Second Avenue, Suite 1401, New York, NY 10017   (212-557-2450)
The liberation movement of Namibia

—Task Force on the Churches and Corporate Responsibility
129 St. Clair Avenue West
Toronto, Ontario, M4V lN5 Canada   (416-923-1758).
An ecumenical coalition to assist churches in implementing policies in the area of corporate social responsibility. Information on divestment, corporations and banks in Canada which do business in South Africa.

—Toronto Committee for the Liberation of Southern Africa
427 Bloor Street, West
Toronto, Ontario, M55 IX7 Canada   (416-967-5562).
Information on liberation movements, anti-apartheid work. Publishes *Southern Africa Report* five times a year.

—TransAfrica/TransAfrica Forum/Free South Africa Movement
545 8th Street, S.E., Washington, DC 20003   (202-547-2550).
A black American lobby on African and Caribbean issues. *TransAfrica Forum* is a quarterly journal of opinion on political, economic and cultural issues affecting black people. Free South Africa Movement coordinates black-led anti-apartheid demonstrations and publicity.

—United Nations Center Against Apartheid
United Nations, New York, NY 10017
Source for detailed documentation and information.

—United Nations Commissioner on Namibia
United Nations, New York, NY 10017
Responsible for implementation of U.N. Resolution 435 when that becomes possible, information on Namibia.

—Washington Office on Africa

Washington Office on Africa Educational Fund
110 Maryland Avenue, N.E.,
Washington, DC 20002   (202-546-7961)
Anti-apartheid Action Hotline: 202-546-0408
A joint office representing legislative and policy interests of a number of U.S. church denominations and religious orders, ACOA and several labor unions. Current information and analysis on U.S. legislative action.

Recent Books on Southern Africa

Some books that have been helpful in preparing *South Africa's Moment of Truth* are listed here. They may be useful to you in further exploration. Those marked with an asterisk and comment will probably be of the most immediate interest. With one exception, all those so marked are published in the U.S. and/or Canada. Ravan Press is a South African publisher whose books are available through Ohio University Press.

Boesak, Allan. *The Finger of God: Sermons on Faith and Responsibility.* Johannesburg: Ravan Press, 1979.

Boesak, Allan. *Black and Reformed: Apartheid, Liberation and the Calvinist Tradition.* Maryknoll, N.Y.: Orbis Books, 1984.

*Boesak, Allan, and Villa-Vicencio, Charles, editors. *When Prayer Makes News.* Philadelphia: Westminster Press, 1986. Essays, documentation on the Call to Prayer for an end to unjust rule.

Bigelow, William. *Strangers in Their Own Country: A Curriculum Guide on South Africa.* Trenton, N.J.: Africa World Press, 1985.

Catholic Institute for International Relations. *South Africa in the 1980s: State of Emergency,* Third Edition. London: CIIR, 1986. Update, No. 4, May, 1987.

Cohen, Robin. *Endgame in South Africa?* Paris : UNESCO, and London: James Curry, 1986.

*Commonwealth Eminent Persons Group on Southern Africa. *Mission to South Africa.*: Hammondsworth, Middlesex, England: Penguin Books, 1986. (Penguin also publishes U.S. and Canadian editions.) An important evaluation by a group of influential moderates destroys the myth of South Africa's reforms and summarizes talks with a range of people in South Africa. Appendix contains Commonwealth Nassau Accord recommending selective sanctions, other documentation.

*Crapanzano, Vincent. *Waiting: The Whites of South Africa.* New York: Random House/Vintage, 1986. Fascinating, well-written account of a year spent with liberal and conservative whites—English-speaking and Afrikaner—in the rural Cape, by a sympathetic American social scientist.

Davenport, T.R.H. *South Africa: A Modern History*, Second Edition. Toronto and Buffalo: University of Toronto Press, 1977.

*Davies, J.G. *Christians, Politics and Violent Revolution*. Maryknoll, N.Y.: Orbis Books, 1976. Theological examination of the issues of violence and revolution in the third world.

*Davies, Rob; O'Meara, Dan; and Dlamini, Sipho. *The Struggle of South Africa*, 2 volumes. London: Zed Press, 1984. Information on the economic and class structure of South Africa and on resistance movement organizations. A socialist perspective.

*de Gruchy, J.W., and Villa-Vicencio, Charles, editors. *Apartheid Is a Heresy*. Grand Rapids: Eerdmans, 1983. Theological essays and reflections on the Reformed tradition in South Africa. Documents from the World Alliance of Reformed Churches and other Reformed church bodies.

*de Gruchy, John W. *The Church Struggle in South Africa*. Grand Rapids: Eerdmans, 1979. Basic information on the history of the churches and the issue of racism, written by a white liberal theologian.

Destructive Engagement: Southern Africa at War. Harare: Zimbabwe Publishing House, 1986.

Elphick, Richard. *Khoikhoi and the Founding of White South Africa*. Johannesburg: Ravan Press, 1985.

Evangelical Witness in South Africa, A Critique of Evangelical Theology and Practice, by "Concerned Evangelicals" of Soweto. Grand Rapids: Eerdmans, 1986. A critique from within the evangelical community of the current evangelical movement in its "apolitical" alliance with apartheid.

Frederickson, George M. *White Supremacy: A Comparative Study in American and South African History*. Oxford, New York, Toronto: Oxford University Press, 1981.

Frederikse, Julie. *South Africa: A Different Kind of War*. Zimbabwe: Mambo Press and London: James Curry, Ltd., 1986.

Gordon, Suzanne. *A Talent for Tomorrow: Life Stories of South African Servants*. Johannesburg: Ravan Press, 1985.

*Green, Reginald H.; Asrat, Direje; Mauras, Marta; and Morgan, Richard. *Children on the Front Line*. New York and Geneva: UNICEF, 1987. A detailed, horrifying account of the effect of apartheid and the *kragdadigheit* war on Southern Africa's children.

Grundy, Kenneth W. *The Militarization of South African Politics*. Bloomington: Indiana University Press, 1986.

*Hanlon, Joseph. *Beggar Your Neighbours: Apartheid Power in Southern Africa.* London: CIIR, James Curry, and Bloomington, Indiana University Press, 1986. South African destabilization and SADCC strategy. A detailed factual account.

Hirson, Baruch. *Year of Fire, Year of Ash.* London: Zed Press, 1979.

*Huddleston, Trevor. *Naught for Your Comfort.* New York: Macmillan Co., 1963. A classic personal testimony by a white prophet.

Innes, Duncan. *Anglo-American and the Rise of Modern South Africa.* New York: Monthly Review Press, 1985.

The Kairos Document: Challenge to the Church: A Theological Comment on the Political Crisis in South Africa, Revised Second Edition. Grand Rapids: Eerdmans, 1986. Very important and controversial theological reflection. The Kairos Document, with some North American responses and study materials, is also included in *The Kairos Covenant* (see the inside back cover of this book).

*Kretzschmar, Louise. *The Voice of Black Theology in South Africa.* Johannesburg: Ravan Press, 1986. An overview of African, Black and Liberation Theology.

Leatt, James; Kneifel, Theo; and Nurnberger, Klaus, editors. *Contending Ideologies in South Africa.* Grand Rapids: Eerdmans, and Cape Town: David Philip, 1986.

*Lelyveld, Joseph. *Move Your Shadow: South Africa, Black and White.* New York and Toronto: Times Books and Random House, 1985. By a *New York Times* correspondent. Compassionate, detailed, vivid account of apartheid from inside South Africa.

Lodge, Tom. *Black Politics in South Africa Since 1945,* London and New York: Longmans, 1983.

Mandela, Nelson. *No Easy Walk to Freedom.* London, Ibadan and Nairobi: Heineman Educational Books, 1965.

Mandela, Winnie. *Part of My Soul Went with Him.* New York: W.W. Norton and Co., 1984.

*Minter, William. *King Solomon's Mines Revisited.* New York: Basic Books, 1986. Well-written, detailed account of how Western policy toward southern Africa evolved after the discovery of minerals.

Mzamane, Mbuelo Vizihungo. *Children of Soweto.* Burnt Mill, Harlow, Essex: Longmans Group, 1982.

North, James. *Freedom Rising.* New York: New American Library, 1986.

*Ormond, Roger. *The Apartheid Handbook: A Guide to South Africa's Everyday Racial Policies*. New York and Victoria: Penguin Books, 1985. Details on how apartheid works and its results; laws and statistics, arranged on a topic-by-topic basis.

Parsons, Neil. *A New History of Southern Africa*. London: Macmillan Education Ltd, 1982.

Seidman, Ann. *The Roots of Crisis in Southern Africa*. Trenton, N.J.: Oxfam America, Africa World Press, 1985.

Skinner, Elliott P. *Beyond Constructive Engagement: United States Foreign Policy Towards Africa*. New York: Paragon House Publishers, 1986.

South Africa, the Cordoned Heart: Twenty South African Photographers. Cape Town: Gallery Press; New York and London: W.W. Norton and Co., 1986. Summary of poverty study by Francis Wilson; details of removals from white areas. Excellent photographs.

Sutter, Raymond, and Cronin, Jeremy. *30 Years of the Freedom Charter*. Johannesburg: Ravan Press, 1986.

Thompson, Carol B. *Challenge to Imperialism: The Frontline States in the Liberation of Zimbabwe*. Harare: Zimbabwe Publishing House, 1985.

Thompson, Leonard. *The Political Mythology of Apartheid*. New Haven: Yale University Press, 1985.

Tutu, Desmond. *Crying in the Wilderness: The Struggle for Justice in South Africa*. Grand Rapids: Eerdmans, 1985.

Tutu, Desmond. *Hope and Suffering: Sermons and Speeches*. Johannesburg: Skotaville Publishers, 1983. (U.S. edition, Grand Rapids: Eerdmans, 1984.)

*Uhlig, Mark A., editor. *Apartheid in Crisis: Perspectives on the Coming Battle for South Africa*. New York: Random House/Vintage, 1986. A useful if uneven set of essays and interviews.

Villa-Vicencio, Charles, and de Gruchy, John, editors. *Resistance and Hope: South African Essays in Honour of Beyers Naudé*. Grand Rapids: Eerdmans, 1985.

Working Women: A Portrait of South Africa's Black Woman Worker. Johannesburg: Sached Trust, Ravan Press, 1985.

Walshe, Peter. *Church versus State in South Africa: The Case of the Christian Institute*. Maryknoll, N.Y.: Orbis Books, 1983.

Walshe, Peter. *The Rise of African Nationalism in South Africa: The African National Congress, 1912-1952*. Berkeley: University of California Press, 1971.

Notes and References

CHAPTER ONE: CRISIS AND KAIROS

1. *The Citizen* (Republic of South Africa), November 23, 1983.
2. *The Star* (Johannesburg, RSA), November 23, 1983.
3. Extracted from a letter in the author's possession dated December 6, 1983. Since the son of the writer is in prison for alleged treasonable offenses, it seems better not to disclose her identity.
4. *Rand Daily Mail* (RSA), September 23, 1983.
5. See *The Citizen*, November 10, 1983; *Rand Daily Mail*, November 12, 1983; *Sunday Times*, November 13, 1983 (all newspapers in the RSA).

CHAPTER TWO: A HISTORY WRITTEN IN BLOOD

1. Neil Parsons, *A New History of Southern Africa* (London: Macmillan Education Ltd., 1982), pp. 5-13.
2. Richard Elphick, *Khoikhoi and the Founding of White South Africa* (Johannesburg: Ravan Press, 1985). See chapters 1-3 for details of the pre-European development of the Khoi-San people into two segments: San and Khoi-Khoi, hunters and herders.
3. Parsons, *A New History*, Chapters 2 and 3. See also T.R. Davenport, *South Africa: A Modern History*, 2d. Ed. (Toronto and Buffalo: University of Toronto Press, 1977), pp. 3-10.
4. See Parsons, *A New History*, pp. 55-71 for details of the Mfecane/Difaqane.
5. For a biography of Moshoeshoe see Peter Sanders, *Moshoeshoe, Chief of the Sotho*, (London: Heinemann, 1975), particularly Chapters 4 and 5. See also Robert C. Germond, *Chronicles of Basotholand*, (Lesotho: Morija Sesuto Book Depot, 1967), a running commentary on the event of the years 1830-1902 by French Protestant missionaries.
6. Parsons, *A New History*, p. 79.
7. Elphick, *Khoikhoi*, Chapters 9-11.
8. Parsons, *A New History*, p. 78-84.
9. Elphick, *Khoikhoi*, pp. 88, 194-200 for early European views.
10. Parsons, *A New History*, p. 82. See Roger Ormond, *The Apartheid Handbook* (New York and Victoria: Penguin Books, 1985), p. 25 for a discussion of the mixed blood of "whites". See also "Miscegenation in South Africa" in Pierre van den Berghe, *Race and Ethnicity* (New York: Basic Books, 1970), p. 224.
11. Davenport, *A Modern History*, p. 25 and Parsons, *A New History*, pp. 87,88.
12. Parsons, *A New History*, pp. 82-88 and Davenport, *A Modern History*, pp. 21, 22.
13. Davenport, *A Modern History*, p. 32.
14. Davenport, *A Modern History*, p. 33-40 and Parsons, *A New History*, pp. 96-100.
15. Parsons, *A New History*, pp. 99-102.
16. Ibid., pp. 102-105. For the mythological significance of the Blood River Covenant and a discussion of whether the Boers were actually impelled by Christian motives and whether the covenant was a real event, see Leonard Thompson, *The Political Mythology of Apartheid* (New Haven: Yale University Press, 1985).
17. Davenport, *A Modern History*, pp. 88, 89. Edward Roux, *Time Longer than Rope*, (Madison: University of Wisconsin Press, 1964), pp. 46-48. Parsons, *A New History*, pp. 109-111, 116, 117. No more than a dozen Africans became voters in Natal.
18. Parsons, *A New History*, pp. 143-200 for the story of the mineral revolution and

the British conquest. See William Minter, *King Solomon's Mines Revisited* (New York: Basic Books, 1986), pp. 9-25 for a discussion of the switch in imperial policy and of structural racism.

19. Davenport, *A Modern History*, Chapters 9 and 10, and Minter, *King Solomon's Mines*, pp. 39-43.

20. Rob Davies, Dan O'Meara and Sipho Dlamini, *The Struggle for South Africa* (London: Zed Press, 1984), Volume 1, pp. 7-11. See also G.V. Doxey, *The Industrial Colour Bar in South Africa* (Oxford: Oxford University Press, 1961), Chapters 2 and 3.

21. Roux, *Time Longer Than Rope*, pp. 101-108; Davies et. al., *The Struggle*, p. 12; Colin Bundy, *The Rise and Fall of the South African Peasantry* (Berkeley: University of California Press, 1979), pp. 204-215, 242.

22. Davies et. al., *The Struggle*, vol. 1, pp. 19,20. See Peter Walshe, *The Rise of African Nationalism in South Africa: The African National Congress 1912-1952* (Berkeley: University of California Press, 1971), esp. pp. 271-281.

24. Walshe, *The Rise of African Nationalism*, pp. 369-370, 401- 405.

25. A full account of the Congress of the People and the Freedom Charter will be found in R. Suttner and Jeremy Cronin, *30 Years of the Freedom Charter* (Johannesburg: Ravan Press, 1986).

26. See Nelson Mandela, *No Easy Walk to Freedom* (London: Heinemann, 1965), pp. 83, 84.

27. Roux, *Time Longer Than Rope*, p. 401. See also Albie Sachs, *Justice in South Africa* (Berkeley: University of California Press, 1973), pp. 214-217.

28. See Roux, *Time Longer Than Rope*, pp. 402-414. See also James Leatt, Theo Kneifel and Klaus Nurnberger, eds., *Contending Ideologies in South Africa* (Grand Rapids: Eerdmans, 1986), pp. 97-101.

29. Mandela, *No Easy Walk*, pp. 185, 188.

30. D. Hobart Houghton, *The South African Economy*, 4th Ed. (Oxford: Oxford University Press, 1976), pp. 182, 183.

31. Baruch Hirson, *Year of Fire, Year of Ash* (London: Zed Press, 1979), p. 3.

CHAPTER THREE: THE CHURCH STRUGGLES FOR ITS SOUL

1. Desmond Tutu, "Spirituality: Christian and African," in *Resistance and Hope*, (Johannesburg: Skotaville Publishers, 1983). See bibliography for U.S. edition.

2. See Neil Parsons, *A New History of Southern Africa* (London: Macmillan Ed. Ltd., 1982), p. 23. For a summary of African religious values, see Kofi Appiah-Kobi and Sergio Torres, eds., *African Theology en Route* (Maryknoll, N.Y.: Orbis Books, 1979) pp. 76, 77. See also Kwesi Dickson and Paul Ellingworth, eds. *Biblical Revelation and African Beliefs* (Maryknoll, N.Y.: Orbis Books, 1969), pp. 24-29.

3. Richard Elphick, *Khoikhoi and the Founding of White South Africa* (Johannesburg: Ravan Press, 1985), pp. 88, 107-109, 205- 207.

4. See Parsons, *A New History*, pp. 90, 95-97, 106, 107 112-13, 121, 125-27, 130, 213-14; Edward Roux, *Time Longer Than Rope* (Madison: Univ. of Wisconsin Press, 1964), pp. 24-32. For a theological critique of liberalism see James Leatt, Theo Kneifel and Klaus Nurnberger, eds., *Contending Ideologies in South Africa* (Grand Rapids: Eerdmans, 1986), pp. 63-65. See John W. de Gruchy, *The Church Struggle in South Africa*, (Grand Rapids: Eerdmans, 1979), p. 12. Chapter 1 gives an overview of South African church history from 1652-1948.

5. See de Gruchy, *The Church Struggle*, pp. 14-18.

6. See Chris Loff, "The History of a Heresy," in John W. de Gruchy and Charles Villa-Vicencio, eds., *Apartheid is a Heresy* (Grand Rapids: Eerdmans, 1983), pp.

10-23.

7. See de Gruchy, *The Church Struggle*, p. 6, 10, 21, 32, 90, 201, 224, in regard to Kuyper, and pp. 18-21 on the founding of NHK and GRK. For an assessment of Kuyper's effect, see Jaap Durand, "Afrikaner Piety and Dissent", in Charles Villa-Vincencio and John de Gruchy, eds., *Resistance and Hope*, (Grand Rapids: Eerdmans, 1985), pp. 39-51.

8. See de Gruchy, *The Church Struggle*, pp. 41-52. See also Itumeleng Mosala, "African Independent Churches: A Study in Socio-theological Protest" in Villa-Vincencio and John de Gruchy, eds., *Resistance and Hope*, pp. 103-111, especially 110-111. See Parsons, *A New History*, pp. 207-212 for details of the movement known as Zionism, the Watch Tower Bible and Tract Society, and the African Methodist Episcopal Church, each of which originated in the United States and had a strong influence in the development of independent African churches. For an estimate of church membership see de Gruchy, *The Church Struggle*, pp. 240-241, and Roger Ormond, *The Apartheid Handbook* (New York and Victoria: Penguin, 1985), pp. 189, 190.

9. de Gruchy, *The Church Struggle*, pp. 53-62, 93; Peter Walshe, *Church versus State in South Africa: The Case of the Christian Institute* (Maryknoll, N.Y.: Orbis, 1983), p. 6.

10. Walshe, *Church vs. State*, pp. 8-10; de Gruchy, *The Church Struggle*, pp. 64-5.

11. The story of the founding and history of the Christian Institute can be found in Peter Walshe's book, *Church vs. State*, which is documented and helpful.

12. Walshe, *Church vs. State*, pp. 111-115.

13. Ibid, pp. 120-121.

CHAPTER FOUR: A SOCIETY DIVIDED AGAINST ITSELF

1. See Roger Ormond, *The Apartheid Handbook* (New York: Penguin Books, 1985), pp. 97-106; *South Africa: The Cordoned Heart* (New York: Norton, 1986), pp. 5-18; Joseph Lelyveld, *Move Your Shadow*, (New York and Toronto: Times Books and Random House, 1985), esp. pp. 132-135.

2. Working Women: A Portrait of South Africa's Black Women Worker (Johannesburg: Sached Trust, Ravan Press, 1985), p. 106

3. Lelyveld, *Move Your Shadow*, pp. 122, 123.

4. Ormond, *Apartheid Handbook*, p. 114.

5. Colin Bundy, *The Rise and Fall of the South African Peasantry* (Berkeley, University of California Press, 1979), pp. 231-235.

6. *South Africa: The Cordoned Heart*, pp. 13, 14.

7. Ormond, *Apartheid Handbook*, pp. 119, 120; *South Africa: The Cordoned Heart*, p. 110.

8. See statement published by Episcopal Church People for the Liberation of Southern Africa and the Western Province Council of Churches (see general information section.)

9. Ormond, *Apartheid Handbook*, p. 9.

10. Ibid., p. 71-76; *South Africa: The Cordoned Heart*, p. 7.

11. See Baruch Hirson, *Year of Fire, Year of Ash* (London: Zed Press, 1979), p. 44-5.

12. Ormond, *Apartheid Handbook*, pp. 77-81.

13. Ibid., pp. 85-89.

14. The status and role of women varied between different African societies. In some cases, women became powerful figures in royal households. Mma-Ntatisi of the Twsana/Sotho clan called the Tkokoa was a military leader while she was acting as the queen-regent for her son, Sikonyela. The Lobedu people

were ruled by a dynasty of rain queens after 1800. See Neil Parsons, *A New History of Southern Africa* (London: Macmillan Ed. Ltd., 1982), pp. 67, 38. The statement in the text is an overall generalization from which one must assume that there were variations, exceptions and departures. See *Working Women*, esp. pp. 15-19, 72-74, 94, 96 and throughout for the effect of the modern economy on women.

CHAPTER FIVE: DOES THE PIPER CALL THE TUNE?

1. *Africa South of the Sahara*, 16th Edition, 1987 (Europa Publications, 1986) p. 911.
2. See Rob Davies, Dan O'Meara and Simon Dlamini, *The Struggle for South Africa* (London: Zed Press, 1984), vol. 1, pp. 51-55; Mark A. Uhlig, ed., *Apartheid in Crisis* (New York: Vintage Books, 1986), pp. 229, 232.
3. See Table: "Leading Items in U.S. Total Exports to the Republic of South Africa in 1986 (1982-1986)" and "Leading Items in U.S. General Imports from the Republic of South Africa in 1986 (1982-1986)." Compiled from official statistics of the U.S. Depart. of Commerce; available in the Department's Trade Library.
4. See Country table for South Africa: "Most Important Canadian Domestic Imports" and "Most Important Canadian Imports into Canada, 1983-1985," summarized from *Imports by Countries* and *Exports by Countries*, Statistics Canada, Ottawa, Ontario.
5. Davies et al., *The Struggle*, vol 1, pp. 56-65. See also Joseph Hanlon, *Beggar Your Neighbours* (Bloomington: Indiana University Press and London: CIIR, 1986), p. 67 and other places. For a detailed account of Anglo-American see Duncan Innes, *Anglo* (Johannesburg: Ravan Press, 1984).
6. Innes, *Anglo*, Appendices 2 and 3.
7. Ibid, p. 234.
8. Uhlig, ed., *Apartheid in Crisis*, p. 232; cf. Davies et al., *The Struggle*, vol. 1, pp. 90, 91.
9. Data is based on BIS survey published April 1987. Uhlig, ed. *Apartheid in Crisis*, p. 243, cites the higher figure. See also also *Africa News*, Sept. 9, 1985, p. 9.
10. *Wall Street Journal*, March 23, 1987; *Christian Science Monitor*, March 25, 1987.
11. Staff Report: "Direct Investment Update: South Africa," U.S. Department of Commerce, International Trade Administration, October 1986.
12. See Testimony of David Hauck, director of the South African Review service of the Investor Responsibility Research Center before the U.S. Senate Committee on Banking, Housing and Urban Affairs, July 15, 1986. 1986 figures are from U.S. Commerce Department, Bureau of Economic Analysis, available on computer tape.
13. *Canada's International Investment Position 1981 to 1984*, Statistics Canada, Ottawa, Ontario, pp. 34, 35, 45. The summary update came from the same source via the Public Information service of the Embassy of Canada, Washington, D.C.
14. *Africa News*, October 22, 1984, based on estimate by Davis, Borkum Hare, a Johannesburg stock dealer.
15. *Value Line Investment Survey*, May 15, 1987, p. 1210.
16. *Federal Reserve Country Lending Survey*, December 1986. The Canadian figure was given to the author by Canadian anti-apartheid sources.
17. See the comments of Prime Minister Verwoerd in 1961 quoted in Uhlig, ed., *Apartheid in Crisis*, p. 242. "Foreign investors look at the stability of the government rather than the policy of the government. . ."
18. Davies et al., *The Struggle*, vol. 1, p. 91.

19. Tom Conrad, in *Bulletin of Atomic Scientists*, March 1986.
20. See *New York Times*, October 26, 1986.
21. See Anne Newman, "The U.S. Corporate Stake in South Africa," *Africa News*, May 20, 1985.
22. See Newsletters 6 and 7 on the "Oil Embargo Against South Africa," published by the Shipping Research Bureau, Amsterdam.
23. Comparisons are based on *Selected Data on U.S. Direct Investment, 1950-1975*, published in February 1982 by the U.S. Commerce Department. The more recent figures show that U.S. investment in South Africa is apparently no longer as profitable as it was in 1964-73. Since 1981, the profitability has deteriorated:

U.S. Rate of Return on U.S. Direct Investment Postion Abroad
(shown in percents):

	1980	1981	1982	1983	1984	1985
South Africa	31.3	19.8	8.4	4.1	-17.0	4.9*
All countries	18.2	14.6	10.1	10.4	10.6	15.2

Source: U.S. Commerce Department: Bureau of Economic Analysis.
* Preliminary data only, subject to change.

CHAPTER SIX: NO EASY WALK TO FREEDOM

1. Nelson Mandela, *No Easy Walk to Freedom* (London: Heinemann Educational Books, 1965), p. 31.
2. Mark A. Uhlig, ed., *Apartheid in Crisis* (New York: Vintage Books, 1986), pp. 202-204.
3. Tom Lodge, *Black Politics in South Africa Since 1945,* (London and New York: Longmans, 1983), p. 336.
4. Ibid, p. 339.
5. Uhlig, ed., *Apartheid in Crisis*, p. 159.
6. Nelson Mandela, *No Easy Walk*, pp. 182, 183.
7. See *Sechaba*, official ANC organ, September 1986, p. 19. The Progressive Federal Party is in favor, apparently, of a so-called confederation of states, but does not favor black majority rule in a unitary state. See John de St. Jorre in Uhlig, ed., *Apartheid in Crisis*, p. 73.
8. See Lodge, *Black Politics*, p. 342.
9. *New York Times*, July 19, 1987, p. 5.
10. *Washington Post*, February 24, 1987.
11. Uhlig, ed., *Apartheid in Crisis*, pp. 156, 157.
12. Ibid, p. 156.
13. *Washington Post*, February 24, 1987.
14. See "We Have Decided to Liberate Ourselves," speech by Oliver R. Tambo on June 23, 1986, to the Royal Commonwealth Society, London, in *Sechaba*, (ANC) August 1986, p. 3, for a discussion of the ANC's position on negotiations.
15. One economist states that voluntary reforms even to bring about black education that is equal to white would take 10 percent of South Africa's national budget and therefore require a sacrifice which is politically unlikely, even if from a Christian point of view such sacrifice is precisely what is required of those who are obedient to God. See Uhlig, ed., *Apartheid in Crisis*, p. 247.
16. See Commonwealth Eminent Persons Group on Southern Africa, *Mission to South Africa* (Hammondsworth, Eng.: Penguin Books, 1986), Chap. 8, pp. 132-3.
17. *New York Times*, May 14, 1987, and January 20, 1987.

18. *New York Times,* January 18, 1987.
19. See James Leatt, Theo Kneifel and Klaus Nurnberger, eds., *Contending Ideologies in South Africa* (Grand Rapids: Eerdmans, 1986), pp. 92, 94 and ff. 23 pages.
20. The political faction was led by Potlake Leballo, who succeeded in ousting the faction led by the military commander, who then formed his own party. After the death of Robert Sobukwe (see Chapter Two) in 1978, factional fighting broke out again. Leballo was ousted and, shortly afterward, one of PAC's chief spokespeople, David Sibeko, was assassinated. In 1981, John Pokela, who had been in prison, was elected to leadership and managed to restore some measure of unity.
21. See Lodge, *Black Politics,* pp. 343, 344; see also Leatt, et al, eds., *Contending Ideologies,* pp. 103, 104.
22. Donald Woods, *Biko* (London: Paddington, 1978), p. 52. For a selection of Biko's writings see *I Write What I Like* (New York: Harper & Row, 1978).
23. See Leatt, et al., ed., *Contending Ideologies,* Chapter 7, "Black Consciousness," pp. 105-112.
24. Ibid, pp. 195, 196.
25. Ibid, p. 116.
26. See *Review of African Political Economy* (No. 35, 1986), for a summary of trade union politics.
27. *New York Times,* June 17, 1986.
28. *Review of African Political Economy,* p. 78.
29. See Leatt, et al., eds., *Contending Ideologies,* p. 115.
30. See Commonwealth Group, *Mission to South Africa,* p. 91.
31. Catholic Insitute for International Relations, (London: CIIR) Update No. 4, May 1987, "South Africa in the 1980's", p. 17.
32. *New York Times,* June 15, 1986.

CHAPTER SEVEN: KRAGDADIGHEIT

1. Quoted in Kenneth W. Grundy, *The Militarization of South African Politics* (Bloomington: Indiana University Press, 1986), p. 11.
2. Ibid., pp. 10-18. Grundy points out parallels in the sense of encirclement of the USSR in the 1920s and the rhetoric of President Reagan and other conservative political figures in the United States against the "evil empire," i.e., the Communist world.
3. Ibid,. Chapter 3.
4. Ibid., pp. 39, 40. Catholic Institute for International Relations, Update No. 4, May 1987.
5. *Washington Post,* June 13, 1986.
6. Abdul Minty in *Destructive Engagement, Southern Africa at War* (Harare: Zimbabwe Publishers, 1986), p. 176. 7. Ibid, p. 177.
8. Grundy, *Militarization,* p. 23, 24.
9. Ibid., p. 29.
10. Ibid., p. 30, 31.
11. Ibid., p. 30.
12. See "Southern Africa: Toward Economic Liberation: A Declaration by the Governments of Southern Africa", made at Lusaka on April 1, 1980. Summarized in Joseph Hanlon, *Beggar Your Neighbours* (Bloomington: University of Indiana Press with CIIR, 1986), pp. 19, 20.
13. See Hanlon, *Beggar Your Neighbors,* pp. 29-31, for a description of a study by

Deon Geldenhuys, commissioned by the Institute of Strategic Studies, University of Pretoria, in 1981. Hanlon argues that Geldenhuys represented the thinking of at least some of the government and the military at the time. My argument proceeds from the actions of the government to destabilize the region and infers motives which are at least consonant with the professed aims of Geldenhuys and such evidence as does exist of a coherent rationale for what is in the end, profoundly destructive and irrational.

14. *Washington Post,* July 29, 1986. Reginald Green, Dereje Asrat, Martha Mauras, and Richard Morgan, *Children in Southern Africa* (New York: UNICEF, 1987), p. 19.
15. See Minty, *Destructive Engagement,* p. 105.
16. Ibid., p. 107.
17. Hanlon, *Beggar Your Neighbours,* pp. 162-167. For a summary of U.S. policy and its involvement in the destabilization of Angola see Cherri Waters, "Destabilizing Angola: South Africa's War and U.S. Policy," published by the Washington Office on Africa Educational Fund and the Center for International Policy., December 1986. WOAEF has also published a profile on UNITA and Savimbi by William Minter (September 1987).
18. Minty, *Destructive Engagement,* p. 28.
19. Ibid., p. 29.
20. See Hanlon, *Beggar Your Neighbors,* Chapter 12, "Mozambique," for details, and Minty, *Destructive Engagement,* Chapter 1.
21. Hanlon, *Beggar Your Neighbors,* pp. 145, 146.
22. Minty, *Destructive Engagement,* p. 36.
23. For details of the plane crash investigation see "Mozambique Information Office News Review," No. 97, January 28, 1987, and No. 105, May 14, 1987.
24. See report of statement by Mark von Koevering, a volunteer working for the Christian Council of Mozambique in "Mozambique Information Office News Review," No. 110, July 30, 1987.
25. See Minty, *Destructive Engagement,* pp. 134-169.
26. Statement of the National Executive Committee of the African National Congress on the Ocassion of the 75th Anniversary of the ANC, January 8, 1987.
27. See SADCC sectoral study, "Mining", presented at the annual consultative conference in Harare, Zimbabwe, January 30-31, 1986.
28. *New York Times,* September 24, 1986.

CHAPTER EIGHT: THE LIBERATION OF THEOLOGY
1. Allan A. Boesak and Charles Villa-Vicencio, eds., *When Prayer Makes News* (Philadelphia: Westminster Press, 1986), p. 29.
2. Ibid., pp. 21-26.
3. John W. de Gruchy and Charles Villa-Vicencio, eds., *Apartheid Is a Heresy* (Grand Rapids: Eerdmans, 1983), p. 59.
4. Ibid., p. 160.
5. Ibid., p. 161.
6. Ibid., pp. 168-172.
7. Ibid., pp. 182-184.
8. Ibid., p. 173. See *New York Times,* October 26, 1986.
9. de Gruchy and Villa-Vicencio, eds., *Apartheid is a Heresy,* p. 90.
10. Boesak and Villa-Vicencio, *When Prayer Makes News,* p. 95.
11. Ibid., p. 150.

12. Ibid., p. 150.
13. Ibid., p. 151.
14. Ibid., p. 133.
15. For a useful discussion of the issue of violence and the use of force from a Christian perspective see Chapter 6, "Violence," in J.R. Davies, *Christians, Politics and Violent Revolution* (Maryknoll, N.Y.: Orbis Books, 1976).
16. See the *Kairos Document*, Revised Second Edition, (Grand Rapids: Eerdmans, 1986) Sec. 3.3, p. 13. On Buthelezi's role see P. Wellings and M. Sutcliffe, "The Widening Rift: Buthelezi, Inkatha and the Anti-Apartheid Politics in South Africa," *TransAfrica Forum*, September 1986.
17. Boesak and Villa Vicencio, *When Prayer Makes News*, p. 130.
18. See Davies, Christians, *Politics and Violent Revolution*, pp. 168-184, for a discussion of the just revolution requirements. For a slightly different version of the just war criteria, see *In Defense of Creation: The Nuclear Crisis and a Just Peace*, by the United Methodist Council of Bishops, 1986.
19. *The Kairos Document*, cited above.
20. See *Evangelical Witness in South Africa: A Critique of Evangelical Theology and Practice by South African Evangelicals*, by the "Concerned Evangelicals" of Soweto (Grand Rapids: Eerdmans: 1986), p. 39.
21. Ibid., esp. pp. 33, 44, 45.
22. See documentation prepared by the World Council of Churches, U.S. Office.
23. See World Council of Churches News Release issued by WCC Communications Office, May 14, 1987.

CHAPTER NINE: WHAT THEN SHALL WE DO?

1. See William Minter, *King Solomon's Mines Revisited* (New York: Basic Books, 1986), pp. 310-319.
2. Se "Why South Africa? Twenty Questions and Answers," by Churches' Emergency Committee on Southern Africa, 1986, p. 14-15, and the "Annual Report 1985-1986" of the Task Force on the Churches and Corporate Responsibility (Canada), pp. 18, 19, for further details.
3. See William Minter, "South Africa: Straight Talk on Sanctions," *Foreign Policy*, Winter 1986-1987.
4. See Elizabeth Schmidt, "The Sanctions Weapon: Lessons From Rhodesia," *Transafrica Forum*, November 1986. A longer version is available from the U.N. Center Against Apartheid: "Lessons from the Case of Southern Rhodesia," by Elizabeth S. Schmidt (87-0334), February 1987.
5. Commonwealth Eminent Persons Group, *Mission to South Africa* (Hammondsworth, Eng.: Penguin Books, 1986), p. 138.
6. World Council of Churches, "Papers from the Meeting in Harare, Zimbabwe, 4-6 December 1985, Response of U.S. Church Leaders."
7. Quotation from the *Johannesburg Star*, September 26, 1985.
8. See Minter, "South Africa" cited in note 3.
9. *New York Times*, June 4, 1987.
10. See Cherri Waters, "Destabilizing Angola: South Africa's War and U.S. Policy," Special Joint Report of the Washington Office on Africa Educational Fund and the Center for International Policy, December 1986, p. 9.